Including Every

Parent

A Step-by-Step Guide to Engage and Empower Parents at Your School
Modeled on a Successful Program at the Patrick O'Hearn Elementary School
By Teachers For Teachers Series, No.8

 PROJECT FOR SCHOOL INNOVATION

Project for School Innovation
197A Centre Street
Dorchester, MA 02124
617.825.0703

www.psinnovation.org

The Project for School Innovation is an initiative of the
Neighborhood House Charter School, a tuition-free public school
serving K-8 students in Dorchester, Massachusetts.

This publication was made possible with support from the US
Department of Education and *The Fund for Nonprofit Partnerships
in Boston Public Schools*. The views expressed in this document are
not necessarily those of the federal government.

ISBN: 0-9716495-7-X

Including Every
Parent

**Developed by Parents and Teachers
at the Patrick O'Hearn Elementary School**

Danette Adams, *Parent*

Kathleen Boyd, *Parent*

Dawn Cunningham, *Teacher*

Amy Gailunas-Johnson, *Teacher*

Kim Sprague, *Parent*

Sharon Williams, *Parent*

with

Ali Bledsoe, *Parent*

Pat Dennehy, *Parent*

Wynne Freed, *Specialist*

Maggie Lodge, *Parent*

Cristina Santos, *Parent*

Christine Tabolt, *Parent*

Edited by

Stefan Lanfer and Kelly Kane

Designed by

Lauren Bessen

Contents

I am very proud of the work O'Hearn teachers and parents have done to make ours a school where close to 100% of families are involved in some way.

From the Desk of Dr. Bill Henderson

September 8, 2003

Dear Reader,

Thank you for your interest in *Including Every Parent*. We all know how important parent involvement is. I am very proud of the work O'Hearn teachers and parents have done to make ours a school where close to 100% of families are involved in some way. I am even more proud of the great impact this has had on student learning and achievement.

Getting to this point has been a journey for the O'Hearn. When I became principal here fourteen years ago, I asked my teachers what their priorities were for improving the school. They had many suggestions, but nearly everyone agreed we needed to do a much better job involving parents and families. Since then, parent involvement has been a priority for all of us at the O'Hearn—for me, for teachers, for specialists, and for existing parent leaders. Along the way, the O'Hearn has developed a number of specific practices that consistently help us recruit, engage, and empower parents. It is our pleasure to share these with you in this book.

As educators, our bottom line is to help students learn and succeed. Working with the Project for School Innovation (PSI) has given us a rare opportunity to help not only our own students, but students at other schools, too. Showing great leadership and dedication, a wonderful team of O'Hearn parents and teachers spent a year working with PSI's highly skilled writers and facilitators to put together this book—researching and exploring what works at the O'Hearn, so that they could share these practices with other schools. Wherever you are on your journey of welcoming, engaging, and empowering families at your school, I hope *Including Every Parent* helps you on your way.

Best wishes,

Dr. Bill Henderson, Principal
Patrick O'Hearn Elementary School

An Introduction to Parent Involvement at the O'Hearn School

The Patrick O'Hearn is well known in Boston as an exemplary elementary school. On standardized tests, O'Hearn students consistently place among Boston's top public schools and above national averages. O'Hearn students shine outside the classroom too—in an arts program that draws national accolades. Under Boston's Controlled Choice Assignment Plan, so many parents rank the O'Hearn as their first choice that all available seats are filled, and many families end up on a long waiting list.

What makes the O'Hearn School so effective, so popular, and so special? One key factor in the O'Hearn's success is that, regardless of the day of the week or the time of day, parents are everywhere—engaged and involved in a wide variety of ways to support teaching and learning at the school. Parents are volunteering at the front desk. They are socializing and strategizing in the family center. They are running a book swap in the hallway. They are directing rehearsals for a talent show in the gymnasium. They are volunteering or substitute teaching in the classrooms. And the list goes on. Close to 100% of O'Hearn parents are involved in the school in some way.

In the 2002-03 school year, a team of O'Hearn parents and teachers worked with the Project for School Innovation (PSI) to better understand how the school is able to involve so many parents so well. The team used PSI's model of action research to uncover the many systems, strategies, and structures that yield such high levels of parent involvement. Then the team tested their findings by sharing ideas with parents and teachers from other schools in the PSI network.

This guidebook provides some of the lessons that came out of this process. It is divided into four sections: *Parents are Present* explores key attitudes and strategies to make sure parents feel welcome and comfortable, so that they want to be present at school. *Parents are Participating* explores strategies for both teachers and veteran family leaders to offer new families entry-level volunteer opportunities—specific, tangible, and manageable tasks—that can lead to more significant involvement down the road. *Parents are Partners* explores strategies for involving parents in ways that directly support teaching and learning. Finally, *Parents are Empowered* examines parents and families in leadership and decision-making roles, taking the initiative to dream up, plan, and execute their own projects to address needs at the school.

Together, these four sections highlight the primary ways parents are involved at the O'Hearn. Many parents do follow them in sequence—first present, then participating, then partnering, then empowered. However, parents can and should be able to begin at any point. A helpful way to visualize a school with a healthy, productive level of parent involvement is as a cycle. Parents can begin at any point, and once parents are in the cycle, they continue to play many different roles.

Effectively involving parents is everyone's job—the principal, teachers, school staff, and parents themselves. As a result, different parts of this book are directed to different parts of this audience. In the early chapters, our step-by-step instructions are directed towards principals, teachers, and veteran parent leaders, whose attitudes and actions can draw new parents into the school as helpers and participants. In later chapters, our instructions are directed more and more to parents themselves, as they are empowered to take on more significant leadership roles.

Including Every Parent is the sixth book in PSI's By Teachers for Teachers series. Through PSI, training and technical assistance are available from the same O'Hearn teachers and parents who developed this book. To learn more about these resources (or about *Including Every Child*), visit PSI's website (www.psinnovation.org) or call 617-825-0703.

• • •

Why Involve Parents?

In most areas of education, there is more contention than consensus—from curricula to instructional strategies to assessment systems. In this book, we explore one education topic about which nearly all researchers actually agree: parent involvement. In recent years, a growing body of research has lined up behind an idea that comes as little surprise to most teachers, principals, and parents—student achievement improves at schools when parents become involved.

Anne Henderson and Nancy Berla summed up much of this research in the opening lines of their 1994 book, *A New Generation of Evidence: The Family Is Critical to Student Achievement:*

> *The evidence is now beyond dispute. When schools work together with families to support learning, children tend to succeed not just in school, but throughout life.[1]*

In 2002, the Southwest Educational

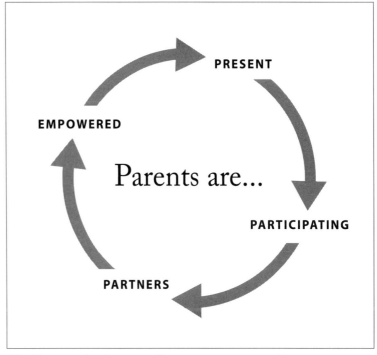

A healthy parent-involvement cycle—many parents engaged in many ways at many times.

Development Laboratory published a review of more recent research on parent and family involvement. According to this report, students whose parents take an active role in their schools are more likely to:

- Earn higher grades and test scores
- Enroll in more higher level programs
- Attend school regularly
- Be promoted, pass their classes, and earn credits
- Have better social skills, show improved behavior, and adapt well to school
- Graduate and go on to post-secondary education

In fact, many researchers also note that family involvement yields such benefits to students regardless of family background or income.[2]

Children are not the only ones who benefit from family involvement. Families and teachers benefit as well. The National Coalition for Parent Involvement in Education (www.ncpie.org) asserts that when student performance improves, it has a positive impact on parents' confidence to help them. Furthermore, it raises teacher morale by decreasing a sense of isolation and increasing a sense of connection to a larger community invested in student success.[3]

At some schools, "parent involvement" is what happens only after students get in trouble. At other schools, "parent involvement" means parents attend a fall open house, they show up for parent-teacher conferences once or twice a year, or they bake cookies or brownies for occasional bake sales.

Family involvement yields such benefits to students regardless of family background or income.

In fact, such activities are only the tip of the parent-involvement iceberg. There are far more, and far more effective, ways for parents to be involved as partners in their children's education. In this guidebook, we explore some of the specific strategies that have worked for us at the O'Hearn.

• • •

Some Guiding Principles for Involving Parents

Running through this guidebook are seven key ideas, attitudes, and priorities that manifest themselves in all of the O'Hearn's efforts to involve parents. Before exploring specific practices in greater detail, we want to draw special attention to these:

1. Prioritize parents
2. Acknowledge parents as the first teachers
3. Bring people together
4. Recognize all contributions
5. Harness multiple abilities and availabilities
6. Use time well
7. Reach all families

1 Prioritize parents

Parent involvement can be successful only if everyone involved remains open-minded, flexible, and truly prioritizes parents. It is one thing for a principal or teachers to say involving parents is a priority. It is another thing entirely to *show* this through actions. If parents can't make a meeting, don't hold it anyway. Reschedule it. Recognize too that, while the principal does play a critical role in welcoming parents and setting the right tone, teachers, secretaries, nurses, janitors, and parents, all share the responsibility for making parents a priority.

2 Acknowledge parents as the first teachers

A successful parent involvement program is built on a foundation of trust. Building that trust begins with teachers. By starting from a place of empathy—by openly acknowledging that parents are the first teachers, and that parenting is possibly the most challenging job there is—teachers can earn that trust, clearly establishing that they are on the same team as parents.

3 Bring people together

Parent involvement begins wherever and whenever parents and school staff come together and start talking. Offering child care, being flexible about when meetings are held, and having a variety of ways for parents to be involved (not just meetings and committees) can all make parents feel welcomed, respected, and valued.

4 Recognize all contributions

At some schools, it seems the only parents seen in a positive light are those consistently present, visible, and vocal at meetings. Yet not all parents are comfortable or capable of playing that kind of role. To engage parents who don't fit this mold, work to create and sustain a positive tone. Don't let parents feel looked down upon, or judged, if they don't come to certain events or aren't involved in certain ways. Instead, ask, "What can we change to make this work for them?" "How can we bring them in?" "How can we welcome them and honor them for whatever contribution they are able to make to the school?"

5 Harness multiple abilities and availabilities

The O'Hearn enjoys a high level of parent involvement because it focuses on utilizing different abilities and talents of different parents. Parents are offered a wide range of events, projects, and meetings to take part in, so everyone can find some place to fit. The school also works hard to vary the times that events take place. Some parents can make a breakfast meeting before work. For others, a lunch, afternoon, evening, or even Saturday meeting may be the only time they have to give to the school.

6 Use time well

Recognize that parents' time is valuable, and be conscious not to waste it. At plays and performances, spend extra time rehearsing the transitions between acts. If you're going to bring everyone together for a show, make sure you pack in the biggest possible punch to the time that they give you. Likewise, at

Sharing samples of a student's work in an after-school parent-teacher conference.

meetings, have agendas, and a facilitator that will help you use time well.

7 Reach all families

As a full inclusion school, the O'Hearn is committed to reaching all children. This commitment extends to families. For family involvement to be truly successful, no family will be left behind.

Seven Goals

What happens when parent involvement is effective? The action research team at the O'Hearn identified a total of seven goals for how they expect to affect parent attitudes, parent actions, parent skills, and school culture. You will notice these goals as a thread strung through all of the practices in this guidebook.

Parent Attitudes

1 Parents feel welcome.

2 Parents feel that their contributions are valued.

Parent Actions

3 Close to 100% of parents are involved in some way.

4 Parents are taking leadership, and decision-making roles.

Parent Skills

5 Parents are educated about curriculum and equipped to help with their child's schoolwork.

School Culture

6 Principals, teachers, and staff feel that parents are their partners in educating children.

7 There is a strong sense of community, a feeling of "family" among parents, teachers, and administrators

Notes

1. Henderson, Anne and Berla, Nancy. *A new generation of evidence: The family is critical to student achievement.* Washington, DC, National Committee for Citizens in Education: 1994.

2. Henderson, Anne and Mapp, Karen, *A new wave of evidence: the impact of school, family, and community connections on student achievement.* Austin, Southwest Educational Development Laboratory: 2002, p. 7.

3. National Coalition for Parent Involvement in Education, www.ncpie.org/AboutNCPIE/AboutPartnerships.html.

Chapter 1

Parents Are Present

Perhaps the plainest indication of a school with strong family involvement is that families, and lots of them, are present lots of the time. In the words of one O'Hearn parent,

> *I've never seen a school where students recognize and know so many parents, and are so excited to see them. All the time I hear, "Hi, Mrs. Sprague!" It's incredible. The O'Hearn is everyone's school, not just the teachers, not just the students, but parents and families too.*

What can principals, teachers, and other parents do to create such a strong sense of welcome? Drawing on lessons from the O'Hearn, this chapter explores four important ingredients to making families feel welcome at the school:

I.   A WELCOMING PRINCIPAL
II. A FAMILY OUTREACH PROGRAM
III. A STRONG WELCOME IN THE ENTRY-LEVEL GRADES
IV. A FAMILY CENTER

tips & ideas

Leave Judgment at the Door

Always lead with the positive. Express your gratitude for parents' time and the hard work of parenting. Find solutions together.

Hold Visitation Days

Set a positive tone with parents well before the first day of kindergarten. Dedicate time to introducing visitors and new families to your school.

A Welcoming Principal

Even though O'Hearn parents and teachers know they all need to work together to support family involvement at the school, they also agree that the principal plays the most significant role in setting a welcoming tone school-wide. Following are five key steps to being a welcoming principal, who makes all families feel comfortable and "at home" at the school:

The Steps

1. Respect parents and focus on the positive
2. Affirm all levels of participation
3. Open the doors with visitation days
4. Be accessible and available
5. Be a familiar face in the classroom

1 Respect parents and focus on the positive

Whenever parents visit your school, start from a place of respect and appreciation for the fact that they took the time to come in. At many schools, parents of children who struggle can be made to feel guilty or ashamed for their parenting. Counter this demeaning tone by focusing on the positive. Rather than blaming parents or making them feel guilty, approach challenges in a collaborative way. Ask, "What can we do to solve this problem together?" In this way, you can make it clear that everyone—parents, teachers, and the principal—wants to see the student succeed. This way, parents can know that they will be heard, and that the school will work with them, as a partner, to develop a good solution for their child.

At the O'Hearn, parents have grown to expect a cheerful greeting from the principal, Dr. Bill Henderson. In fact, Dr. Henderson's greeting is often so warm many parents feel that their coming to the school is the best part of his day. In the words of one parent, "Dr. Henderson always seems to leave judgment at the door. You could have had a kid here for four years and never been to the school. When you walk in, the first thing he says is, 'I'm so happy to see you.'"

2 Affirm all levels of participation

At some schools, there are only a few ways for parents to be involved. This makes it easy for a small group of highly visible, highly vocal parents to dominate. Meanwhile, other parents seem to be forgotten—parents who are less outspoken, parents whose time is more limited, or parents who feel overwhelmed by their more vocal peers. Allay these concerns by explicitly affirming all levels of participation. Don't dismiss or grumble about parents who are less visible or less involved. Don't suggest they do not care about the school. Instead, start with the assumption that all parents care deeply about the school, and their children's success. Every parent's circumstances are different. Some simply have more time than others. Ask yourselves, "How can we make this work for them? How can we bring them in?" One O'Hearn parent put it this way, "People work different shifts. For me, it just so happens that sometimes I can come to events or meetings. But that's not true for everyone, and it's really easy to forget that."

3 Open the doors with visitation days

Make it clear that parents are welcome at your school by opening your doors to them before they even decide to enroll their children. Host visitation days for prospective parents. Visitation days can introduce parents to your school and teachers, while also demonstrating how much you value and welcome families. Walking into the O'Hearn, parents are met by a colorful, multilingual sign that reads, "Welcome." Many O'Hearn families see this sign for the first time when they arrive as visitors for an O'Hearn visitation day.

tips & ideas

Know they Care
Assume that all parents care deeply about their children's success at school, and that they want to be involved.

As they walk through the doors of the O'Hearn, a colorful banner reminds parents that they are welcome.

Opening doors, without compromising learning or safety

At the O'Hearn, both parents and teachers boast of the school's "open door policy." In almost all circumstances, parents are welcome as volunteers, as extra pairs of hands on projects, and as supporting adults working with small groups of students in classrooms. At the same time, schools must be smart about their open doors. This is something staff at the O'Hearn have learned over time. Initially, the school had a very casual policy towards visitors. And while it was certainly more the exception than the rule, a few parents abused this privilege—consistently coming in late and interrupting classes to deliver things to their children. Schools must also weigh safety concerns.

With these things in mind, the O'Hearn, while remaining a school that welcomes and celebrates family involvement, adopted a more strategic visitor policy. Except at the beginning and end of the school day, when multiple O'Hearn staff supervise the pick-up and drop-off of children, parents are required to check-in at the front office before visiting their child's classroom. We also ask that parents arrange class visits in advance with their child's teachers. On visitation days, all visitors receive a set of simple guidelines, which affirm that they are welcome in all classrooms, but set boundaries—such as numbers of visitors, length of visits, and protocol for speaking with teachers—that keep learning from being interrupted. *See Guidelines for Visitors in Appendix, page 72.*

At least one Friday each month, Dr. Henderson opens the doors of the school to parents and families of potential future students, and others interested in learning more about the O'Hearn. He gives a short introduction, answers questions, reviews some simple guidelines for visiting classes, and then encourages visitors to see as many classrooms as they'd like (*See Appendix, page 72*). Sometimes he'll accompany families as they walk. One O'Hearn teacher shared her perspective on how visitation days help set a positive, welcoming tone for families at the school:

> *A lot of the faces I've ended up seeing here, I saw first on visitation days. Dr. Henderson shows them around and introduces them. He's recruiting them really. "This is so and so," he'll say, and then add all kinds of nice things about a person he's met and spoken to for maybe ten minutes, "And they have a very nice little girl who is thinking about the school."*

Visitation days mean a lot to parents, too. One O'Hearn parent compared her first experience of the O'Hearn with that of another school she visited:

> *When I first came to the O'Hearn, I was just visiting the school with my son to see if it would be a good fit for him. I went to the Kindergarten classroom, expecting to spend maybe twenty minutes tops. Forty-five minutes later, I hadn't been asked to leave, nor was I made to feel in any way that I'd worn out my welcome. By contrast, when I visited another school, it was cold as ice. I went into a Kindergarten classroom, and the teacher said, "You can look. Don't touch."*

4 Be accessible and available

It's one thing for a principal to say, "Parents and families are welcomed and valued at our school." It's another thing for them to show it. Parents can easily tell the difference. If a parent comes in, and you're not in (or racing off to) a meeting or dealing with a crisis, take a moment to speak with the parent. Don't hide behind a secretary or a date book.

If an O'Hearn parent would like to speak with the principal, they don't necessarily need an appointment. In the words of one O'Hearn parent,

> *It isn't like many schools, where if you want to talk to the principal, you call and leave a message. And if you hear back at all, it's the secretary saying, 'He might be able to squeeze you in for 15 minutes next Tuesday.' Simple things like that really put a parent off.*

5 Be a familiar face in the classroom

A principal plays a key role in setting a tone where parents feel welcomed at the school. Nevertheless, it takes a lot of work for that welcoming tone to flow from the principal's office into teachers' classrooms. Help your staff to trust you and your vision for parent involvement by becoming a familiar face, a regular visitor in different classrooms, and not only when it is time for formal evaluations. On a typical day at the O'Hearn, Dr. Henderson visits three or four classrooms. After these visits, he offers informal, positive feedback, and develops a warm rapport and a sense of trust with his teachers. In this way, teachers can feel comfortable and at ease when he opens their doors to parent visitors.

A principal can't merely impose an open-door policy, and expect family involvement to soar. One O'Hearn teacher put it this way:

> *The staff needs to buy in. A principal can't just say, 'You're going to let parents into your class all the time.' He or she has to build trust first, so that we don't feel like we're always being judged.*

tips & ideas

Take Time to Win Staff Buy-In
Be a familiar face and a faithful cheerleader. Build trust with your staff, to put them at ease about opening the doors of their classrooms to families and visitors.

A second banner in the O'Hearn entry way highlights the school's emphasis on inclusion. All students and families are valued here.

tips & ideas

Make a personal connection on their home turf

When parents visit parents in their own living rooms, it provides a tangible, personal connection for parents that might be intimidated by schools and teachers.

Bring food and don't be *all* business

When planning home visits, include food. This facilitates socializing and community building.

A Family Outreach Program

For many families, schools are intimidating places. Becoming involved, and getting to know other families at a school can often seem overwhelming, especially for families that don't speak English as a first language. One important tool to address such challenges is a family outreach program. At the O'Hearn, a family outreach team, made up entirely of parent volunteers, goes out into the community and welcomes new families into the larger O'Hearn family, from the comfort of their own living rooms. Members of the family outreach team give out books and information about the school. They talk about ways parents can be involved. And they answer any questions the new families may have. Before the school year even begins, families getting ready to send a child to the O'Hearn for the first time can expect a call, *and a visit* from another O'Hearn parent. A family outreach program is not difficult to set up, and it isn't a great deal of work, but it offers a big pay-off in terms of making new families feel welcome. One O'Hearn parent described her visit by an outreach team member,

> *It made me realize my children were at the right school. We had come to a visitation day, and I loved what I saw. But I really wanted something concrete, some personal contact with someone. Then I got that visit. It reassured me that we'd made the right choice for our child. I was able to ask a lot of questions. It was the first time I heard about the family center. I was used to just getting phone calls.*

The Steps

1. Assemble an outreach team
2. Identify a coordinator
3. Throw a planning party
4. Develop a standard home-visit protocol
5. Visit new families
6. Follow up

1 Assemble an outreach team

As a first step in setting up a family outreach program, assemble a parent outreach team. If your school already has an existing parent-leadership team, team members might simply recruit additional parent volunteers through a letter home, a note in the school newsletter, an announcement at a school-wide event, a posting on the school website, a group e-mail, or some combination of the above. Otherwise, work with your staff to generate a list of parents from diverse backgrounds, who they consider to be good candidates for leadership. Approach each of these parents individually and invite them to be part of a family-outreach team.

2 Identify a coordinator

As a group, nominate a coordinator or pair of coordinators. Overseeing the family outreach program does not entail a massive amount of work. Still, it is important that one or two parents step forward to be in charge of it, and to take primary responsibility for each of the following steps—to make sure that home visits happen in a timely and effective way.

3 Throw a planning party

When there is a large enough core of parent volunteers, gather together for a planning party, to assign and plan home visits. In preparation for this planning party, contact the principal to get the names and contact information for all new families. Contact entry-level grade teachers for suggestions of materials to share with new families, and collect enough copies for visitors to distribute. At the O'Hearn, we bring a copy of our reading contract, some leveled books, and a school phone list, which includes contact information for key school personnel, as well as parents in charge of recruiting parent volunteers.

What constitutes a sufficiently large "core" of volunteers depends on how many new families your outreach team aims to visit. In a typical year at the O'Hearn, we have about twenty new families. In the first year we had a family outreach program, we had a total of fifteen volunteers. This meant each volunteer visited one, or at most two families, which worked very well. In some years, we have done home visits with fewer volunteers. However, in our experience, home visits work best when there are enough volunteers so that no one has to visit more than two families. Visiting three or more different families becomes time intensive. It also makes follow-up more difficult. If, by the time you gather for a planning party, your group is still small, spend some time coming up with names of other parents to recruit.

As with most O'Hearn gatherings, a planning party typically includes food—usually a barbeque or potluck picnic. This way, the team can socialize and enjoy the warm summer weather, as they get down to business.

4 Develop a standard home-visit protocol

As a group, discuss how you will approach the visits, what materials you'll bring, and what key information to share. Review the list of new

tips & ideas

Divide and conquer
Recruit enough volunteers so that no one has to visit more than two families. With more volunteers, no one is overwhelmed, and follow up can be more effective.

tips & ideas

Follow up with a phone call

A home visit is a great first connection, but don't stop there. Follow up with a phone call to makes it clear you are serious about welcoming new families to your school.

families and divvy up the names. Distribute books and other materials for visitors to hand out. Set deadlines for completing the visits, and establish a simple system for letting the coordinator(s) know when visits have been made. At the O'Hearn, we do this simply with a phone call or e-mail. If team members have done visits before, invite them to share what worked well, and any challenges they encountered in the past. Decide on a basic process for visits that all volunteers can use as a guide. The final two steps we describe here outline the basic process every visitor follows at the O'Hearn.

5 Welcome new families

Call each family you were assigned, introduce yourself, and arrange a time to drop by. When you do visit, introduce yourself again, and talk about children you have at the school and any ways you have been involved there. Ask about their children. Share books and materials you have brought with you. Describe important features of the academic program. Mention some of the ways for parents to volunteer and be involved. At the O'Hearn, we generally kick off the year with a new-parent breakfast. Home visits are a great time to remind new families about this event. Invite new parents to share any questions or concerns. Leave your phone number, in case they think of anything later.

6 Follow up

Within a week or two of your visit, whether or not the new parents have called you, give them a call to say, "Welcome to the school family," yet again. Find out if they have any more questions. And let them know you hope to see them at the school's fall open house and/or any other special kick-off events.

Let Us Show You

ASSEMBLING A FIRST FAMILY OUTREACH TEAM AT THE O'HEARN

tips & ideas

Even though close to 100% of O'Hearn families are now involved in the school in some way, this wasn't always the case. Dr. Henderson became principal of the O'Hearn in 1989. That fall he surveyed his teachers to find out what they considered to be the school's biggest challenges. **A** Many teachers mentioned parent involvement—more specifically the lack of it—at the O'Hearn. As a first step to address this challenge, Dr. Henderson invited teachers to come up with a list of parents, from diverse racial and socioeconomic backgrounds, who might serve as leaders of an effort to involve more parents. Following this discussion, Dr. Henderson personally invited ten parents to be founding members of a committee to involve more families at the school. **B**

This simple approach—generating a list of parents and inviting them all to serve as leaders—proved very effective. Soon after this parent leadership team first gathered, they decided to begin making personal, one-on-one, parent-to-parent home visits, as a way to welcome and draw in those families that almost never came to the school. **C** To do this, the family involvement committee assembled a group of parent volunteers, called the family outreach team. Using word of mouth, notices in the *O'Hearn Star* (the school newsletter), and letters home, the committee drew together a diverse group of fifteen volunteers. **D**

In this first year, the family outreach team made personal visits to families that almost never came to the school. Over time, many of these same families began to be more involved. Building on this success, the family outreach team decided to use this approach whenever a new family joined the O'Hearn community. In this way, the team reasoned, they could set a positive, welcoming tone with all families from the very beginning of their experience with the school. **E** Home visits began to occur every fall, starting in the 1992-93 school year.

A Don't just dictate that teachers must welcome parents. Build staff buy in by inviting their ideas.

B Start with a core of diverse parent leaders, nominated by teachers, and personally invited by the principal.

C Parent-to-parent home visits provide a highly personal, un-intimidating way to welcome new families to your school.

D Get the word out any way you can.

E Home visits within the first few weeks of school set a tone for new families that they are not alone, that they are welcome at the school, and encouraged to be involved.

tips & ideas

A Parents are sometimes intimidated by schools and teachers. No one can help ease those concerns so well as another parent.

B Home visits are for extending personal, warm welcomes to school, invitations to be involved, and to answer questions. They are not for lectures, guilt-trips, or demands to volunteer.

C Positive family-involvement experiences often lead to even more family-involvement. Parents on the receiving end of home visits one year can be recruited to visit new parents the next year.

Let Us Show You

A HOME VISIT

Kim Sprague's oldest daughter was about to start kindergarten at the O'Hearn. Kim had heard wonderful things about the school—it was the family's top choice when they submitted their preferences for the Boston Public Schools' lottery. Still, Kim was a little nervous—what parent wouldn't be? So, when she received a call from Delores Handy, another O'Hearn parent, offering to stop by and talk about the school, Kim gladly accepted. **A**

Something about that name: Delores Handy. Kim couldn't place it, but it seemed familiar. The following week, when Delores came by, Kim put the pieces together.

"Hi, Kim. I'm Delores Handy."

"Oh, my gosh!" Kim recognized the voice. "I know how I know your name. You're Delores Handy from the radio. WBUR. I listen to your show all the time!"

"That's me," said Delores. "That's my day job—actually my early-morning job. The rest of the time, I'm a mom. I've got twins—a boy and a girl—who are now in the third grade at the O'Hearn."

"Wow. That's great."

"This year, I'm part of the family outreach team. We like to stop by, just to say hello, and to welcome new families to the O'Hearn. **B** I've brought some materials and information. If I could just come in for a few minutes, I'd love to share it with you."

"Sure, sure," said Kim. "Of course. Come in. Wow, this is so great. You are so nice to come."

"Oh, I'm happy to," said Delores. "It wasn't so long ago, I got my first visit from an O'Hearn parent. We really are a big family. Who knows? Maybe next year, you'll be knocking on some stranger's door. **C** I know what it's like sending a first child to a new school. It's nerve-wracking."

"It's silly, I know," said Kim. "I've heard nothing but what a great place the O'Hearn is. But still…you're right. I worry about how she'll do there."

"It's not silly at all. The O'Hearn is a special place. But she is still your baby. And you want the absolute best for her. All parents at the O'Hearn—maybe all parents everywhere—feel the same way. At the O'Hearn, parents show it by pitching in all the time, in all sorts of ways, to help the school be the best it can be for our kids."

"Well, I definitely want to learn more about that."

"Great. Great. I wanted to tell you about are some of the ways you can be involved. And as I mentioned, I've brought a few things—some

important phone numbers at the school, and of other parents, some information about the home reading program, and a few books. **D**
I also want to make sure you know about the new parent breakfast next week, and the family center...but before I go into any of that..."

"Wow, that's a lot." Kim seemed a bit overwhelmed.

"Don't worry," Delores assured her, "I'll walk you through it all pretty quickly now, but if you have questions you can always call me later. I'll leave you my phone number." **E**

"Thank you. That would be great."

"Well, first and foremost, tell me if you have any questions you've been dying to ask."

"I do actually. I've been trying to find out...you see, my daughter really likes..." And another home visit was under way, another new family welcomed to the O'Hearn.

tips & ideas

D Bring information and materials on home visits.

E Relationships are the fuel that drives family involvement. Share family contact information, so that those relationships can grow and develop over time.

Parents hold an impromptu discussion about next year's home visits.

tips & ideas

Get them from the get-go

Teachers of entry-level grades play an enormous role in making parents feel welcomed and valued. Take a proactive role in welcoming new families at the beginning of their time at your school.

A Strong Welcome in the Entry-Level Grades

Finding ways to make families feel welcome and to involve them at a school is everyone's job. The principal, all teachers, other parents, the school secretary, the nurse, and even the janitor help to set this tone. However, since they are the first teachers parents get to know well, it is extremely important that teachers of students in entry-level grades be especially welcoming. These first encounters do a lot to shape families' expectations and attitudes about their children's school. At the O'Hearn, most students begin their journey in Kindergarten, where teachers Paul Murphy and Dawn Cunningham use a number of simple, effective strategies to welcome and involve new families.

The Steps

1. Send a welcome letter
2. Start the year with a visiting day
3. Keep parents plugged in with a class newsletter
4. Use multiple forms of communication
5. Develop simple tools to track parent requests
6. Celebrate milestones together
7. Welcome help of any kind

1 Send a welcome letter

Before school begins, set a positive tone by sending a welcome letter to parents of students new to the school. By the time students are enrolled at the O'Hearn, many of their parents have already been to an O'Hearn visitation day. Many of them have already met and spoken with the Kindergarten teachers, Ms. Dawn and Mr. Paul. Either way, come August, Paul and Dawn send out a welcome letter to all parents. This includes some basic information about the start of the school year, items children will need for the first day, a phone number parents can call with questions, and a short questionnaire for parents to fill out. The questionnaire is designed as a tool for parents to communicate important information about their child, such as speech or language difficulties, health issues, prior experiences in playgroups or in other school settings, information about siblings, etc. The questionnaire also invites parents to indicate if and when they would be interested in volunteering in the classroom.

2 Start the year with a visiting day

The day before the official first day of school, host a visiting day for families new to the school. In this way, you can establish from the very beginning that parents are welcome at the school, and in your classroom. Each year at the O'Hearn, on the day before the first day of school, the Kindergarten hosts a visiting day. From 9:30 AM until noon, families are invited to visit the classroom with their children. This is a chance for them to meet (or re-meet) Ms. Dawn and Mr. Paul. As they get acquainted with the school and the classroom, parents can ask questions of the teachers. They can also begin getting to know each another. Relationships are the fuel that powers parent involvement. With a visiting day at the very beginning of the year, families can start building those relationships from the very beginning of their time at a school.

Dear Families,

Welcome to Room 6! We are excited about this upcoming school year and are looking forward to working with you and your children!

As you may already know, our first day of class is Monday, September 9, 2002. However, we would like to welcome you to a **Visiting Day for New Families** on Friday, September 6, 2002 between the hours of 9:30 AM – 12:00 PM. This will be a good time for you and your child to familiarize yourselves with the school, classroom and teachers. Both of us will be available to answer any questions or concerns you may have.

We would also like to ask that you send in the following things with your child on the **first day of school**:

_____ **A name tag (piece of tape or sticker) on their shirt, so they can be easily identified in the classroom or when they get off the bus. **VERY IMPORTANT**

_____ Backpack – Large enough to hold a large book (approx. 9"x12") (labeled with their name).

_____ Extra set of clothes, including: shirt, pants, underpants, socks, etc. (also labeled) in a labeled plastic bag.

_____ A snack (forms will be sent home to determine your child's eligibility for free or reduced price school snack).

We hope to see you on Friday, September 6th for the Visiting Day! *If for some reason you have decided not to send your child to the O'Hearn School this year, please notify the school immediately, as we have a long waiting list.* Thank you for your help. If you have any questions, you can reach either of us at 617-635-8725.

Sincerely,

Paul Murphy
Dawn Adams

A beginning-of-year letter from the kindergarten classroom announces visiting day and welcomes parents to the school.

A Team Effort to Cross Language Barriers

At the O'Hearn, and especially in Kindergarten, teachers strive to reach all parents. One year, parents of a student in Kindergarten were incredibly difficult for teachers to reach. As recent immigrants from Vietnam, language barriers made communication difficult. They rarely responded to requests from the school, and they were not participating in the school's home reading program (a parent-involvement tool we'll discuss in greater detail in chapter three). As a result, the child was beginning to lag behind his peers.

Midway through the year, through conversations with their colleagues, the Kindergarten teachers learned this student had a cousin—a fifth grader at the O'Hearn—who lived in the same apartment building. This older student was much further along in her language skills, so the Kindergarten teachers asked for her (and her parents') help connecting with the family of the child in their room. As a result, communication improved remarkably. The student's parents were present at more classroom events, and they regularly responded to requests from the school—like completing a weekly home reading contract.

tips & ideas

Reach all families

Some families will always be harder to reach than others, particularly with language issues. Be creative! Recruit older students, cousins, uncles, or neighbors as translators, who can serve as bridges between your school and the harder to reach families.

March Newsletter 2003
Room 6

A Wonderful Celebration!!!

On Thursday, February 13th, we celebrated our 100th Day of Kindergarten with a party. Almost all of our students and their families attended. Thank you to everyone for bringing in all of the delicious food. Most children brought in a collection of 100 things to add to our party. Many of those collections are still on display in our classroom. If you

FAMILY COOKING

At our party, a few families signed up to come in and do a simple cooking project with us. **If anyone else is interested in cooking with us, <u>please let us know</u>.** *There is plenty of time available to add more people to the list.*

Sensory Motor Area

On Monday mornings, the

A classroom newsletter keeps parents informed about ways to be present, like the 100th Day party.

3 Keep parents plugged in with a class newsletter

Send a periodic classroom newsletter from your entry-level classrooms, so that parents can stay "plugged-in" all year. All O'Hearn families receive a copy of the O'Hearn Star, a school-wide newsletter that is explored in greater detail in the next chapter. Parents of children in Kindergarten also receive their own newsletter, which focuses exclusively on their children's classroom. Ms. Dawn and Mr. Paul use this newsletter to share all kinds of important information and to make sure all families can feel connected to everything that is going on in the classroom. The Kindergarten newsletter highlights student birthdays, special events, parties, and also a wide range of information about curriculum—songs, sign language, numbers, and games students are learning in school, so that parents can practice with them at home.

4 Use multiple forms of communication

Letters and newsletters are one good form of communication, but don't rely on them alone. Strong communication between teachers and parents is built upon the widest possible variety of types of communication. Not all parents can be reached in the same way. Families that don't speak English as a native language might struggle to understand even a simple, two-page newsletter, or a note from a Kindergarten classroom. Be creative. Try e-mail. Try telephone calls. Try speaking with parents as they drop off or pick up their children. Take advantage of other family members and other families.

5 **Develop simple tools to track parent requests**

Every parent has a favorite way to communicate with teachers. Some like to leave hand-written notes in their children's backpacks, or in teachers' mailboxes in the front office. Some parents prefer verbal communication—leaving phone messages, or in person at the beginning or end of the day when they drop off or pick up their child. Still others prefer e-mail. To track all of these different requests, develop one simple, consistent system to record and respond to messages, no matter how they arrive. At the O'Hearn, Ms. Dawn and Mr. Paul use a simple, low-tech message system by following these steps: Post a small dry-erase board (or chalkboard) on the classroom door. Whenever you get a message from a parent—be it paper, verbal, or electronic—simply write it on your message board. At the end of each day, review your messages. Erase the ones you've dealt with, and attend to the ones still pending.

6 **Celebrate milestones together**

With a visiting day at the beginning of the year, you began building parents comfort with the school and their relationships with each other. Continue to build on this with celebrations and special classroom events throughout the year, where parents can participate, socialize, and have fun together. One of the biggest parts of the math curriculum for children in Kindergarten is counting the days of Kindergarten. Each day, students count how many days they have been in school, and their teachers add another large number onto the wall around the classroom. When students reach the 100th day of kindergarten, we celebrate by hosting a potluck lunch party. Every family brings some food and we celebrate

tips & ideas

Throw parties with food

Teachers in the upper-level grades often focus on involving parents in ways that support academics. In entry-level grades, focus simply on bringing parents into the school and making them feel comfortable. A potluck party is a great way to do this.

Students and their families celebrate the 100th day of kindergarten.

tips & ideas

Recognize any contribution

Acknowledge even the smallest efforts. Expressing your gratitude often pays off in parents' enthusiasm to do more in the future.

together with music, dancing, and games. Typically, nearly all of the Kindergarten families attend this party, making it a great opportunity for families to socialize, to deepen relationships with other O'Hearn families, and to grow steadily more comfortable and at home at the O'Hearn. Other teachers and school staff also stop by to share in the fun and all the great food. In this way, parents of Kindergarteners get to know and be known by even more members of the O'Hearn family—in many cases, the teachers their children will have in years to come.

7   Welcome help of any kind

Acknowledge and welcome help of any kind, so that parents know they are appreciated and valued. When you show gratitude for small things, parents get excited about helping out again, often playing more significant roles. If you acknowledge only the big stuff, many parents may feel too intimidated to try—worried that their time or their talents are too small to make a difference. Throughout the O'Hearn, parents are encouraged to help in any way, shape, or form that they can. In the words of Principal Bill Henderson,

> We work on honoring whatever contribution parents are able to make. We recognize that some parents work three shifts. Some can help in one way. Some can help in another way. Everybody has different levels and ways they can contribute. At the O'Hearn, just getting kids dressed, and ready, and off to school every day is an enormously valued contribution.

Teachers in entry-level classrooms play an incredibly important role in establishing this tone. From there, if all teachers share this attitude, parent involvement can thrive school-wide. At the O'Hearn, parents' first encounters with the school are characterized by a wide-open welcome. They hear it from other parents on the outreach team. They read about it in the summer welcome letter from the Kindergarten. They hear about it in conversations on visiting day, and in ongoing, informal interactions all year long. The Kindergarten teachers work especially hard to welcome and encourage parents to be involved however they can be—helping with special events, like the 100th day party, painting the room, gathering supplies for projects, or even just being an extra adult in the classroom once a week, once a month, or even just once! Every bit helps.

Family Center

For many O'Hearn parents, their first connection to other O'Hearn parents happens in their own living rooms with a home visit. Parent-to-parent interactions don't end there, however. All year long, every year, O'Hearn parents can meet with other parents in the O'Hearn family center. The family center is a place where parent can meet, drink coffee, share breakfast, relax, socialize, and ask questions of other parents—questions they might feel less comfortable asking a teacher or administrator, or questions another parent can give them the best possible answer to. For parents of a special-needs child, for instance, no one can help them understand what their child's journey through school will be like better than another parent whose special-needs child is a few years further along. The family center is open to families at most once a week, and at least once a month. In time, the O'Hearn family center has become parents' living room away from home. Following are six basic steps for creating a family center at your school:

The Steps

1. Dedicate a space
2. Spread the word
3. Provide coffee and food
4. Welcome children
5. Enjoy time with other parents
6. Invite guests with expertise

1 **Dedicate a space**

The first step in starting a family center is to find a space for it. If, like the O'Hearn, your school has literally no rooms (or even closets) to spare, think about what rooms could be transformed into a family center at certain dedicated times each month. A small school in a small building, the O'Hearn was stretching its seams before anyone even thought of creating a family center. Parents might have enjoyed having a space exclusively for them, but that has never been a practical option. Instead, the school has given parents specific spaces at dedicated times. Initially, the family center was held in the library every Friday morning. When the school needed the library to start doubling as a computer center, this ceased to be feasible. With no other free room left in the school, the family center might have folded. But O'Hearn teachers

tips & ideas

Ask and answer
Make your family center a place for parents to raise questions and, now and then, to get them answered by special guests with relevant expertise.

tips & ideas

Coffee, food, and kids

Provide food and welcome children, so that all families can attend. Don't expect parents to wake up early, feed their children, and hire a baby sitter to attend a family center.

Parents and teachers at work developing this book. Children are a welcome addition.

weren't willing to let that happen. It was clear to them how much families valued having time and space to congregate, relax, and speak with other parents. So, even though a dedicated faculty room is written into all of their contracts, teachers agreed to share their special space with families one Friday morning every month.

2 Spread the word

Once you have a space and time set aside for the family center, spread the word, or else no one might show up to enjoy it. At a small school like the O'Hearn, we rely a lot on word of mouth to get the word out. But we also make sure that the date and time for the family center is listed on the school calendar, and also that it gets mentioned in our school newsletter, the *O'Hearn Star*.

3 Provide coffee and food

Develop a rotating list of parent volunteers who can share responsibility for providing coffee and food. At the O'Hearn, we have found this simple touch helps to draw parents in to the family center. It also helps them feel comfortable and at ease while they're there. The O'Hearn holds family center first thing on Friday mornings, 9:15-10:30 AM. Each time we open the family center, a different parent takes responsibility for setting up coffee, bagels, and donuts.

4 Welcome children

Welcome children at your family center, so that all parents and families can attend—not only those without young children or those who can afford babysitters. As with almost any O'Hearn function, children of all ages are welcome at the family center.

5 Enjoy time with other parents

Now that you're together, enjoy coffee, food, and the company of your fellow parents. Ask questions. Share ideas based on your experiences at the school. Discuss challenges you've noticed, or school projects you think could use some extra hands. Brainstorm ways that parents could take the initiative to improve things.

6 Invite guests with expertise

Often, questions, challenges, and concerns parents raise in the family center can be answered by other parents who have been at the school longer. However, if questions come up that go beyond the expertise and experience of other parents, be creative about inviting different experts in as guest speakers. At the O'Hearn, we often invite specific teachers and the principal to visit the family center. We also routinely invite visitors from outside the school. In one family center gathering, a number of parents of 5th graders raised a lot of questions about what would happen after their children graduated. At the next family center, a representative from Boston Public Schools stopped by to answer questions about what students' transition to middle school would be like.

tips & ideas

Be creative with space

Don't be deterred by space constraints. Cafeterias, libraries, gymnasiums, even faculty rooms can – for a few hours each month – be dedicated for parents.

March 2003
Patrick O'Hearn School

Monday	Tuesday	Wednesday	Thursday	Friday
3 Book Swap / Learning Disabilities Presentation Gr. 4/5 / *PSI Focus Group 3:45-4:30 p.m.	4 School Based Management 4:00 p.m.	5 Math Coach Grades 2 and 3 / Officer Buchanan Grades 3/5	6 Dances from India 1:15 and 2:10 / Math Coach Grades 2 and 3	7
10 *PSI Focus Group 3:45-4:30 p.m.	11 Room 3-Visits Zoo	12 Tchr. Wkshp 8:00 a.m. Writing/Science / Officer Buchanan Grade 5	13	14 African American History Show 2:05
17 Evacuation Day / NO SCHOOL	18	19 Math Leadership Team 8:15 a.m. / Literacy Coach Gr. 4/5	20 Visitation Day 9:45 a.m. / Instructional Leadership Team 8:00 a.m.	21 Family Center 9:15 a.m. / Second Term / Marks Close
24 Book Swap / *PSI Focus Group	25	26 Literacy Coach Gr. 4/5	27 Math Family Night	28 Visitation Day 9:45 (PSI)

A monthly calender keeps parents in the know about ways to be involved.

Chapter 2

Parents Are Participating

I n the last chapter, we discussed a number of ways we work to establish that parents are welcome at the O'Hearn. In this chapter, we explore the next layer of parent involvement, where parents are not only present, but also *participating* as volunteers and helpers in a wide variety of special events, projects, and activities.

To help parents and families make the jump to this deeper level of involvement, teachers, staff, and veteran family leaders offer new parents a wide range of ways to volunteer. We come up with many small, specific, "starter" tasks that are very manageable. When new parents take on these small but significant responsibilities, they experience success, positive recognition, and deep satisfaction from making a contribution to the school. This often leads to more significant involvement, even leadership, down the road.

In this chapter, we explore three important tools that help us recruit and engage parents as participants at the school. These are:

I.   PARENT VOLUNTEERS
II.   A SCHOOL NEWSLETTER: *THE O'HEARN STAR*
III. A TALENT SHOW

tips & ideas

Match supply and demand with a survey

Use a simple survey of teachers and parents to identify and match needs for help with interest in helping.

Parent Volunteers

At many, perhaps most schools, parents want to be involved, to offer their skills, their talents, and their insights to support their children's learning. Likewise, at most schools, dedicated, hardworking teachers would like nothing more than to have an extra pair of hands. However, it isn't always so clear how to make the connections between parents' desire to help and teachers' need for it.

At the O'Hearn, the principal, teachers, and staff all share the view that parents care a great deal, and that they are every bit as concerned about their children as the school is. Starting with this assumption, O'Hearn parents and teachers have generated some simple, yet effective, ways for effectively recruiting parent volunteers.

The Steps

1. Survey teachers
2. Survey parents
3. Compile results in a binder
4. Assign simple, specific, *necessary* roles
5. Follow up
6. Support ongoing, open communication

1 Survey teachers

In the first or second week of school, develop a simple survey asking teachers to list specific projects and activities that they are planning, and for which parent volunteers would be useful. Include a space for teachers to estimate the amount of parent volunteer time each project will take. Work with the principal to determine the best way to give surveys to all teachers. Perhaps the principal will ask teachers to complete the survey in the last five minutes of a staff meeting. You might leave copies in teachers' mailboxes, and set out a collection box in the front office, where they can drop them off. However you get surveys into teachers' hands, set a deadline of no more than one week later for them to return them to you, so that you can move the process forward.

2 Survey parents

When teachers are finished, compile all the information and use it to create a simple survey for parents. (*See Appendix, page 73*) List all the different projects parents could help with, and a rough estimate for how much time each project would require. Invite parents to review all of these, and to put a check mark beside any they are interested in working on. Leave extra space for parents to indicate additional interests, skills, and talents they would like to offer the school. At the O'Hearn, a group of two or three parents works together to develop, administer, and process these surveys. When parents have completed their surveys, they return them to this group of parent coordinators. Once again, in order to establish urgency, and to keep this process moving, set a deadline of no more than one week after parents receive surveys.

3 Compile results in a binder

Collect the data from the teacher and parent surveys into a binder that is available to all teachers and all parents. At the O'Hearn, this binder is kept in the front office. Whenever a teacher is planning a project and could use some support, she can flip through the binder to see which parents have applicable skills and interests. This way, she can know which parents would be the best ones to approach about volunteering. Likewise, parents who have ideas for their own projects can use the binder to recruit other parents to help them (see *Parent-Initiated Projects*).

Keep in mind that your parent volunteer binder is a tool to help identify parents who *might* like to be involved—parents who can be high on your list of people to call as possible volunteers. Make sure that parents always feel comfortable saying, "No." Just because s/he is a skilled painter or seamstress, no parent should be relied upon to paint every set for every school play or to sew all the costumes.

4 Assign simple, specific, necessary roles

Keep it simple. Come up with as many clear-cut, specific, manageable assignments as you can. This way, parents won't feel intimidated. They will also be able to see that they are getting things accomplished. When a parent says, "I can't do that. I don't have the time (or the skills, or the patience, etc…)", tell them, "You can do as much or as little as you want." Make it clear that all contributions are important and appreciated. When parents take on and complete a simple, specific, manageable task, they can realize, "Oh, I can do that!" In our experience, such discoveries often inspire parents to become even more involved. One O'Hearn parent was first involved as a visitor to the family center. Then she started volunteering to prepare food and coffee. With consistent encouragement and affirmation from teachers and fellow parents, she steadily took on more responsibility. Now, this same parent is co-director of both the after-school program and the annual Talent Show.

tips & ideas

Keep asking, keep offering, and keep talking

Effectively involving parents is an ongoing effort, built on one-on-one conversations between parents and teachers or parents and other parents, through notes home in kids' backpacks, or through notices in the school newsletter.

Start small

When you first recruit parents, provide a range of small, un-intimidating tasks and assignments—making phone calls, folding programs, or setting up chairs. These can be gateways for more significant involvement down the road.

tips & ideas

Assign necessary tasks
Trust parents with necessary tasks. "Busy work" wastes parent time and teacher time, and it is a strong disincentive for future involvement. Have higher expectations for parents. Give them real opportunities to support teachers and students.

Make fundraising work for you
With parent-initiated fundraisers like a talent show, you're not just raising money, but also welcoming, recruiting, and empowering parents as leaders, and creating opportunities for students to shine.

Make sure the roles you assign are not only specific and manageable, but also necessary, so parents know that their efforts are valuable. Sometimes teachers worry that parents may not follow through and complete tasks. Acting out of this skepticism, teachers may assign tasks merely to keep parents busy—where it doesn't really matter whether parents finish them or not. While such a strategy may alleviate teachers short-term concerns, in the long term, it can only undermine parent involvement. If parents, eager to volunteer, are given meaningless "busy work," it wastes their time and teacher time. What's more, it is a strong disincentive for them to volunteer again.

5 Follow up

In addition to making tasks manageable, make sure that you follow up with your new volunteers and celebrate their contributions. In part, this can be a check-in to make sure the projects are being done. More importantly, it is a chance to cheer on and give praise to new volunteers.

6 Support ongoing, open communication with and among parents

The more parents are in communication with one another, the more ways they find to be involved with the school. Since the O'Hearn is a small school where parents feel very comfortable with one another, much of this happens informally, by word of mouth, with fliers sent home in children's backpacks, or through phone calls. Other more structured tools like the *O'Hearn Star* (a parent-written school newsletter), the family center, parent and school-based management meetings, and a parent e-mail listserv all help to facilitate a free exchange of ideas and information. Ample advance warning for meetings and events is also very important. Parents should not hear for the first time on a Wednesday that they must make a plate of cookies or brownies for a bake sale on Friday.

HELP WANTED!!
One or Two Days December 20th and January 6th-10th
TO ORGANIZE COSTUMES FOR PLAY.
NO EXPERIENCE NECESSARY

We Need Help!

Do you have articles or information you'd like to share? Do you have writing, computer, graphic, photography or other skills you'd like to put to use?

Join us. Kenny and Delores love doing this Newsletter but we'd like to make sure everyone else who wants to work on it has an opportunity as well.

A snapshot from the *O'Hearn Star*, recruiting parents as participants.

A School Newsletter

THE *O'HEARN STAR*

S uccessful parent involvement at any school depends on strong communication—parent to principal, parent to teacher, parent to parent. At a small school like the O'Hearn, where parents are so often *present*, much of this communication can happen informally. However, the reality for many parents is that, regardless of their interest or desire to be present at school, they simply do not have time to spare. Keeping these parents connected is important, too. This is why the O'Hearn community depends so heavily on our monthly newsletter, the *O'Hearn Star*.

Each month, all families get a copy of the *O'Hearn Star*, which is completely organized, edited, printed, copied, and distributed by a dedicated team of parents. In the words of one parent, the Star is an "O'Hearn institution. If I ever want to know what's going on, I just look in my kid's backpack for the *O'Hearn Star*." It gives parents a forum to get the word out about important events and to recruit parent volunteers for different projects. Teachers display student work. And anyone who has them—the principal, teachers, specialists, or parents—can share updates, ideas, and advice with the entire school community.

In this section, we describe the key steps to developing and sustaining this vital resource:

The Steps

1. Decide what to include
2. Identify parent editors
3. Develop systems to collect information
4. Collect student work
5. Divide and conquer
6. Let students distribute

1 Decide what to include

As a first step in creating a school newsletter, decide what you want it to include. Certain features of the *O'Hearn Star*, however, are almost always the same. There is always a letter from the principal ("From Dr. Henderson"), from the creative arts team ("Moves"), from the nurse

tips & ideas

Include student work

A school newsletter is a great forum for sharing student work. With a simple, rotating schedule, teachers can share this responsibility and have plenty of time to prepare. Also, by the end of the year, every classroom can have a chance to display their work.

tips & ideas

Identify parent editors

To generate a consistent, high-quality newsletter, identify parent editors. Running a newsletter is a big job, but parents can do it any time of day that is convenient for them.

("Nurse's Notes"), and there are always samples of student work. Other items vary with each edition. Editors always leave room for new announcements about special events, notes from teachers or parents looking for volunteers, or even phone numbers for local legislators, whom parents can call to defend the school budget. Many editions of the *Star* also include pictures and reports about recent school events. With all of these pieces, a typical *O'Hearn Star* is between 10 and 14 pages long.

2 Identify parent editors

Rather than making your newsletter yet another responsibility for teachers or administrators, harness a great opportunity to involve and empower parents as leaders. Identify two or three parents to serve as co-editors of your newsletter. One of the reasons the *O'Hearn Star* is read so eagerly and faithfully by everyone at the O'Hearn is that so many parents, school staff, and students contribute to each edition. With all of these contributors, it would be easy for the newsletter to become an unwieldy, inconsistent mess. But at the O'Hearn, two parents act as Editors-in-Chief, which means they are responsible for recruiting submissions, setting deadlines, assembling articles, doing the layout and design, printing, copying, and distributing copies. The co-editors don't generally do all of this work themselves. They recruit other volunteers to help with different parts. However, thanks to their leadership, the school has a new edition

---

To: Teachers, Staff and Parents:

The **DEADLINE** for the November edition of the ***O'HEARN STAR*** is Wednesday, <u>November 20, 2002.</u>

Please send your articles, photos, drawings, graphics, etc. to Delores Handy Brown via George or Lauren in Room 8, or to Kenny Rae via e-mail at <u>ohearnstar@hotmail.com</u>.

You don't have to wait until the deadline to make your submissions. Please send them in as soon as possible. The sooner you get them to us, the better.

If you have bits of information or notices that you'd like to have included in the newsletter, but find you don't have time to write the article, call me (Delores) at ▮▮▮▮▮▮▮, or pull me aside when you see me at school. I'll make sure it gets in the newsletter.

A monthly notice, calling for submissions to the *O'Hearn Star*.

of the *Star* by the end of the first week of virtually every month. The layout of the *O'Hearn Star* is relatively simple, but we have found it is helpful if at least one of the newsletter co-editors has the skills to do basic layout and design work.

3 Develop systems to collect information

Develop simple, reliable systems for parent editors to collect information for your school newsletter. This will make it a truly effective—inclusive and comprehensive—tool for communicating important information. Keep your newsletter on track by setting and sticking to strict deadlines. Each month at the O'Hearn, parents, teachers, and staff get a reminder notice from the *Star* co-editors. The note tells them when the next submission deadline is, and it also describes all of the different ways to submit things for publication. These include: speaking directly to one of the two parent co-editors; leaving messages with the co-editors' children, leaving notes in a mailbox in the front office set aside for the *O'Hearn Star*, or sending an e-mail to one of the co-editors.

4 Collect student work

Create a system for classroom teachers to submit student work, so that you can showcase students demonstrating success in their academic work. At the O'Hearn, we are always looking for ways to publicly display and celebrate the academic work of our wonderful children. The *O'Hearn Star* offers an excellent way to do just that. The final pages of each edition of the *Star* are always dedicated to student work. At the beginning of the year, classroom teachers sign up on a simple, rotating schedule indicating when they will submit samples of their student work. This gives teachers plenty of advanced warning and plenty of time to think about and choose what they will share. Once teachers have chosen work, they submit it to the parent editors. What teachers submit is entirely up to them, and they often involve students in the decision. Sometimes teachers submit drawings, sometimes essays or poems, and sometimes math problems. Students get the thrill of seeing their work, and the work of their peers, in print, and parents get to see their students be successful at school.

5 Divide and conquer

Collecting information, doing the layout, printing, copying, and distributing a newsletter, all within monthly deadlines, is a big job. Try to avoid the temptation to let one or two "superstar" parents shoulder all of this responsibility. Recruit additional volunteers, who can be responsible for different parts of the newsletter—collecting student work from teachers, making sure the principal gets his or her note in on time, doing the layout, printing and making copies, or sorting them and putting them in

tips & ideas

Share the Work

Don't ask your editors to do everything every month. Even if other parents can only help with one edition, recruit them to share different tasks like collecting materials, making copies, and passing them out to teachers.

tips & ideas

Make it an honor to carry it home

Save time, money on copying, and mailing. Trust the eldest child in each family with the honor of bringing home the school newsletter.

teachers' boxes. However you divide up the tasks, many hands can certainly make lighter work of this relatively big job.

6 Let students distribute

However good a school newsletter, however well packed with useful information, if nobody sees it, writing it is a waste of time. Some schools print newsletters that languish in piles in their front office, picked up and glanced at only by occasional parents or visitors. Other schools add the costly, and logistically complicated step of doing a mass mailing of newsletters to families. At the O'Hearn, we simply count on the oldest students from each family to bring a copy home. Not only does this become an honor for them (an honor that younger siblings are thrilled to take on once their older siblings graduate), it also saves us time and money—fewer copies, fewer *wasted* copies, zero mailing costs, and zero time to address, lick, or stick envelopes. At the beginning of the year, one or two parents work together to make a list of all the oldest students, and how many of them are in each class. This way, every month, parents in charge of distributing the *O'Hearn Star* simply refer to this master list and distribute the appropriate number of copies to each class.

The O'Hearn Star   *January 2003*

The Newsletter of the Patrick O'Hearn School Family Center

"I have the audacity to believe that children everywhere have the right to three meals a day for their bodies, education and culture for their minds, and freedom, justice and equality for their spirits"

Martin Luther King, Jr.
Nobel Peace Prize Ceremony.
Oslo, Norway.   December 10, 1964

Stop the Cuts
message   *back page*

Inside..

B for Biography pics

Important message from Dr. Henderson

January Moves

Keep warm with Nurse Pat's advice

Safety tips form BPD

Attention All Parents!!!

Will our children be denied the opportunity to learn if the proposed budget cuts are implemented?

Two weeks ago O'Hearn parents met in an emergency meeting to discuss the cuts being proposed in response to the Superintendent's mandate that all schools submit plans that would cut their budgets by 10%. Over thirty parents attended the meeting. All agreed that the proposed cuts would be devastating to our school as well as other public schools.

What can we do? We have formed a number of committees as we begin to oppose these cuts. Our committees include outreach and media. If you are interested in working with us or if you would like to be kept informed of our efforts, please send a note to the office. You may also send in your e-mail address if you are interested in being contacted by e-mail.

At this point we are focusing our efforts on reaching out to other organizations and other public schools. Using our **Stop the Cuts** paper as a reference, we hope to contact as many people as possible to help spread the message.

"All budget cuts hurt. We must fight for our schools and our children"

Please call the elected officials below and let them know how you feel. Let them know that as a concerned public school parent you:
"are angry and disturbed at the impending cuts"
"are concerned that these cuts will undercut efforts to improve our schools" "will not support cuts to education"

Feel free to use any of the points in our **Stop the Cuts** paper on the back page to support your argument. Finally be sure to let them know where you live and that you are watching to see if they will support our schools.

STATE REPRESENTATIVES
Thomas Finneran-Speaker-Dorchester/Mattapan -617-722-2500
Gloria Fox-Roxbury- 617-722-2692
Shirley Owens-Hicks- Dorchester/Roxbury/Mattapan 617-722-2256
Angelo Scaccia-Hyde Park/Roslindale 617-722-2692
Marie St. Fleur-Dorchester/Roxbury 617-722-2060

A typical coverpage of the *O'Hearn Star.*

The O'Hearn Star

February 2003

The Newsletter of the Patrick O'Hearn School Family Center

Date to Remember!
March 14th
Join us for the African American History Show highlighting contributions of great Americans who played a pivotal role in building and shaping this country.

Beached whales on Centre Street!? Page 8

Should we have zoos?
Room 10 Fifth graders debate the topic. Pages 6-8

Mr. Brand-Budget Casualty?

One of the proposals being considered as Boston Public Schools move to slash at least 10% across the board from next year's budget is one that could cost us our custodian. The plan reportedly would eliminate custodial positions at small schools which have only one or two custodians. They would be replaced by private contractors. A contract with an outside firm could create major problems! Consider this-the BPS would be hiring contractors. The contractors could bring anybody in! Would the people change from day to day? How often would they come? This is just one of the many unreasonable proposed solutions being offered in an effort to solve the budget crisis.

We cannot afford this! Mr. Brand is part of the family, the fabric of life here at the O'Hearn. Think of all the ways he goes beyond the call of duty to help create the sense of community we have here at the O'Hearn. His birthday show alone makes the case for him. If you haven't seen it, ask your children to tell you about it.

Keep up the Pressure!

Parents, you've done a wonderful job of coalescing around the "Stop the Cuts" movement, but we still have a lot of work ahead. Governor Mitt Romney has said he wants to spare education from his budget cutting ax. But has he? He's reducing local aid to cities and towns. That will most likely filter down to budget cuts for schools. Keep making those calls and sending those letters. Make sure the decision makers on Beacon Hill and at Court Street hear us!

School Based Management Meeting Tuesday, March 4th at 4:00pm.

Topics on the agenda: Budget Update; Plans to stop smoking advertisements that appear right in front of the O'Hearn School; Museum of Fine Arts grant; Military Moms/condiment drive; and more. You can attend the meeting or offer input through your

---

We Need Help!

Do you have articles or information you'd like to share? Do you have writing, computer, graphic, photography or other skills you'd like to put to use?
Join us. Kenny and Delores love doing this Newsletter but we'd like to make sure everyone else who wants to work on it has an opportunity as well.
ohearnstar@hotmail.com

Attention Jazz Lovers and Performers!!!

Do you love to blow that horn? Think you can blow like Satchmo? Or even Myles? Tickle those ivories like The Duke? Or Count? Do you ever feel you'd just like to pretend you're Ella, Sarah, Peggy, Carmen, Nancy, Rosemary, even Ole Blue Eyes? Well, have we got a forum for you!!!

The O'Hearn After School Program is looking for ADULT jazz performers (musicians and singers) for a jazz show in February. The show will be a fundraiser for the After School Program. For more information contact Sharon Williams 617-635-

Stop the Cuts

- We are parents of children in the Boston public schools and we oppose school budget cuts. School budget cuts will undermine the gains that have been made over the past several years. You cannot expect children to meet high academic standards and then take away the support they need to achieve in the classroom.
- Most schools do not have frills or extra programs that can be cut to save money. Cuts mean fewer teachers, and fewer teachers mean a big drop in the quality of education. Cuts also mean the elimination of programs like art and music that keep youngsters engaged in school.
- Many cuts will end up costing the school system more money. Special education students have Individual Education Plans (IEPs) that serve as contracts. When conditions in the classroom change, parents have the right to reconvene their IEP teams and consider alternative placements.
- **MCAS** is a contract that will be broken if funded inadequately. Governor Romney and legislative leaders must justify their support of MCAS in light of the budget cuts they say are necessary. At what point do school budget cuts deny students the opportunity to learn and thus make the MCAS graduation requirement unfair, illegal and immoral?
- Despite the current budget crisis, Massachusetts faces a long term teacher shortage. Budget cuts will force younger teachers out of the profession, wasting all the money that has gone into training them and leaving the next generation of students without experienced teachers.
- Political leaders have rallied behind the rhetoric of "No Child Left Behind." These cuts will leave a whole generation of public school children behind. State leaders should not be allowed to say they support education and then refuse to raise the revenue necessary to support the real work. This may mean new increased taxes dedicated to education.
- Parents cannot stop supporting their children for a year or two because times are tough. They have to make sacrifices in other areas and raise the money necessary because you cannot get the years of childhood back at some later date. Government officials should be held to the same standard.

Books that Children *and* Parents Love

It's always wonderful when you find a book that both your children and you love! So often, I find that I love a book and they could care less about it, or they want to hear something a million times that I find incredibly boring or poorly written. So I thought I would list books that both my sons and I love---maybe your children would like them too!

The Little House by Virginia Lee Burton.
This wonderful book, written in 1942, tells the story of a small house in the country that slowly becomes surrounded by urban sprawl and forgotten and ill-cared for. Finally, it is found by the descendants of the original owners and moved back to the country. The pictures are so detailed and fascinating, and it's so amazing to kids that the same house can stay in the same place while the surrounding change so drastically!

Bus Route to Boston by Maryann Cocca-Leffler.
This is a great one for Boston residents! It's about a trip on a bus into the city to do and see things we can still do and see today---go to Filene's Basement, get an ice-cream sundae, buy produce at Haymarket, etc! It's so exciting to my boys to see T buses like ones we actually go on, and I love seeing houses that look like the one we live in and around! So many books are set in worlds that are imaginary or far from our real life, and it's nice to read a book set in the city we actually live in!

I'd love to know which books are the favorites of other families! Happy Reading!!

More book recommendations from Suzanne Amara next month.

Children's Safety is Priority #1

- Don't Drive Fast. Be aware of the flashing 20mph lights during school hours.
- Tell your children to heed the directions of the School Traffic Supervisors. They are hired to get our children safely from one side of the street to the other.
- Teach your children how to cross on their own, show them how to use the lights, and to always look-LEFT-RIGHT-LEFT to make sure it is clear and continue to look as they are crossing.
 If there are walkers, encourage them to NOT walk alone (a group is always safe) and if they do, make sure that the school is aware of that as well as the School Traffic Supervisor (they are excellent for watching out for our children).
- Teach them to watch out for cars that might be backing up, listen for engines, please don't talk to strangers. If this does happen make they tell you, the parent, the teacher, the principal, the school traffic supervisor the police.

Remember that early morning and late afternoon traffic does not last long, so be patient.

This Traffic Safety Notice came from Boston Police Officer Linda Lyons, the Advisor for the School Traffic Supervisors of Area C-11 the District which polices the section of Dorchester around the O'Hearn School.

"B is for Biography. It's also for Beautiful and Brilliant."

We say "Amen" to those remarks by Dr. Henderson at the conclusion of the spectacular stage show and musical performed by O'Hearn students in grades K-3. Through a wonderful series of short performances, complete with sets and scripts based on the lives of notable historical figures from Marian Anderson to Louis Braille, to Seiji Ozawa, they put on a show that was entertaining and educational.
The show offered a snapshot of some of the wonderful work of Ms. Saba and other members of the Arts team. Our children sang their hearts out and performed like pros. From the opening song with students from Rooms 5 and 6, to the Symphony Orchestra with actual string instrumental performances by Room 8 students, to Room 2 students acting out a play based on a book by Eric Carle, it was a spectacular success. Thank You Ms. Saba and all the cast members from Grades K, 1, 2 and 3. We loved

---

My School is Beautyful
Kevin

Do you really want to know what makes my school beautyful? Well let me tell you. First of all we are all equal. No one gets left out of anything like kickball or plays. We always have a good time.

We are like family. We do things together. We help others. We are all different in our own way. I'm in a wheelchair. People help me by getting my things. I'm excited when people help me. It makes my life easier when I get help.

If we work together nothing is too complicated. O'Hearn School is *beautyful!*

The Beautyful O'Hearn
Jake

Hi. I go to a very kind school. The Patrick O'Hearn School. This school has a lot of different kids and teachers. The teachers at the O'Hearn School are very kind to help all children. They take the time to help us with our school work. Because of the teachers, our school is perfect. Well almost. Some of the children at the O'Hearn School are not capable of some things that some other children can do. But they are very kind in many ways.

My school is very beautyful and by reading this essay I wrote, I hope you think so too!!

Why my school is so Beautyful
Maggie

I think my school is so beautyful because it lets disabled or not disabled kids here. We are not separated in different classes like some schools. We have ramps so the people in wheelchairs can get up. Everyone respects everyone else even if they are disabled. My teachers call on everyone.

As I walk down the halls I see people laughing together. They are not making fun of each other. They are sharing a joke together. Disabled, not disabled, they are having fun together. They are my friends. My

Why My School is Beautyful
Atiba

Why my school is beautyful is because we have different color students. We have smart kids. We respect each other. We take turns to help in the morning. Our teachers are smart and generous. We have good books to read. The O'Hearn is the best school to go to. The O'Hearn is a beautyful place to be. I like the O'Hearn School a lot.

Why I Like the Patrick O'Hearn
Raees

Why I like the Patrick O'Hearn School is because of the teachers, Peace Day, independent reading, and Recess. The teachers are not so good; the teachers are not so bad; they're just right. Peace Day is good because it's just peace all day, having fun, making necklaces. Independent reading is good because you need to read once a day. Recess is good because you need to get fresh air from doing all that work.

The other thing I like about this school is the equality. Nobody is left out, even if they've got disabilities. This school's perfect!

My Beautyful School!!!!
Jeanine

In my beautiful school they let all kids go on stage especially kids that are in wheelchairs. There are people like Kiwi, Kevin, and Olivia. They treat us like we are all a family. There are also good teachers to help us. They always give us pizza or cake if we all do something good. In our school there are many kind children. They let us do plays and have independent reading. We do not judge people on how they look. There are many accessibilities for children of all abilities. This is why my school is beaufiful!

More samples from the *O'Hearn Star*.

tips & ideas

Share the director's chair
Don't rely too much on any individual parents. In a talent show, or any big event, encourage parents to share the directors' chairs.

A Talent Show

At the O'Hearn, parent involvement really helps the performing arts to thrive. Our highly talented arts team produces as many as four or five major productions with music, dance, and dialogue, each year. These shows offer many opportunities for parents to volunteer as helpers and supporters, even if that support is simply helping their children learn and practice their lines or dance steps. Even with all of these outlets for their dramatic and musical talents, O'Hearn students are still bursting at the seams to put more of them on display. Responding to this obvious desire, a group of parents began what became an annual tradition at the O'Hearn—the Talent Show, which is developed and run entirely by parents, making it an ideal opportunity to recruit parents as participants at the school. The O'Hearn Talent Show has become a truly wonderful event, a special opportunity for the entire O'Hearn family to come together and celebrate its children.

The Steps

1. Identify parent co-directors
2. Recruit and identify talent
3. Get double permission
4. Rehearse and focus on transitions
5. Advertise
6. Capture the memory of performances

1 Identify parent co-directors

To put on a talent show of your own, start by identifying parent co-directors. A talent show creates opportunities for many parent volunteers, because there are so many different jobs to do, such as creating costumes, building and painting sets, overseeing rehearsals, and helping with the transitions between acts. All are critical to the success of the show, so it is helpful to have a team of two or three parents who can share the responsibility of overseeing them all.

Running a talent show is a big job, so, try not to let any one parent shoulder it alone. This is often easier said than done. Even at the O'Hearn, where close to 100% of our parents are involved in some way, certain parents do tend to take the lion's share of the big jobs. In some years, one or two parent have literally "run the show" themselves, and

O'Hearn Talent Show Rehersal Schedule
3:30 - 4:30 pm

MONDAY	THURSDAY	FRIDAY
March 10	April 17	March 14
March 32		March 28
April 7		April 4
April 14		April 11

Dress Rehersal Thursday, April 28, 2003

A typical rehersal schedule for the O'Hearn talent show.

tips & ideas

Treat it as a privilege
Students should get permission from both parents and teachers to indicate they have earned the privilege of participating.

Include everyone
Find ways to include everyone, whatever their "talent"—standing on their head, doing somersaults, whistling, or stuffing marshmallows into their cheeks.

they almost always do a super job. Nevertheless, we have learned that just because these incredible parents rarely say, "No," there is no excuse for asking them to do everything. Keep in mind that your goal of involving parents in a talent show is not only to put on a good show, but also to get a number of parents involved—not just a few powerhouse leaders.

2 Recruit and identify talent

Use fliers, newsletters, and word of mouth to recruit talent (and interested students possibly unaware of their talents). Set a date and time when all students interested in participating stay after school to meet with the parent director (and co-directors) and any other parent volunteers this core group is able to recruit. (*See arts performance materials in Appendix, pages 74 and 75.*)

As a full inclusion school, the O'Hearn has an impressively broad notion of what constitutes talent. For the O'Hearn Talent Show, we believe if you want to participate, you have a talent, even if you don't know what it is. Maybe it's juggling, standing on your head, doing cartwheels, jumping up and down, reading poetry, or some creative combination of the above. Some kids will arrive knowing exactly what they want to do. For others, the team of parent volunteers helps students identify talents they can share.

tips & ideas

Use time well

Short acts. Quick transitions. Large casts. If parents sacrifice time to see a show, pack as many kids (and as much talent) into the time they give you.

3 **Get double permission**

Get permission from parents and teachers. Make sure interested students get permission slips (at the O'Hearn we print them on the back of our fliers), where both parents and teachers sign off on their participation. At the O'Hearn, being in the Talent Show is a privilege reserved for students who have been doing their work and behaving in class.

4 **Rehearse and focus on transitions**

Teacher, principal, and parent time is precious. If you're going to bring everyone together for a show, make sure you give them an opportunity to see as many students as possible, in as short a time as possible. Otherwise, you may be in for a lot of staring at closed curtains, and parents impatiently checking their watches, while they wait for the next scene or act to be ready. At the O'Hearn, we usually rehearse the Talent Show eight or nine times, for an hour after school, with one dress rehearsal on the last day before the show. At rehearsals, we particularly focus on the transitions between acts, so that they can be quick and fluid by show time. We emphasize this at all arts performances at the

O'HEARN TALENT

PARENT / TEACHER PERMISSION FORM

Student Name _____ Grade /Rm _____

Parent Name _____ home # _____ Work # _____

Emergency Contact Person _____ Phone# _____

PARENT

I give my child permission to participate in the Talent Show. I understand that I must make arrangement for my child to be pick up after each rehearse by 4:30pm and by 8:25pm the night of the show. I also understand that my child must continue to be in good academic standing to remain an active participant in the show. I realize that my child must demonstrate respect toward both staff and other performs. Disrespectful or disruptive behavior will not be tolerated. I understand my child will not be allowed to continue participating in the show if he/she exhibiting this behavior.

_____ _____
PARENT SIGNATURE   DATE

TEACHER

I acknowledge that the above student is in good academic standing. I feel that this student will be able to remain in good academic standing while participating in the show. I agree to contact the staff if this student academic standing changes due to his/her participation in the show.

_____ _____
TEACHER SIGNATURE   DATE

Treat participation as a privilege with a double permission form.

The billboard for an O'Hearn arts performance.

tips & ideas

Make a video
Help parents and students relive the fun of a show with a video. This way parents who couldn't make the show can also see their children shine.

O'Hearn, because it relates directly to one of our primary goals for family involvement—use time well.

5 Advertise

In the same ways you recruit talent, use fliers, newsletters, word of mouth, and notes stuffed in backpacks to recruit your audience. (*See arts performance materials in Appendix, pages 74 and 75.*)

6 Capture the memory of performances

Lights, curtain, action! Watch your students shine, and celebrate them together with the rest of your school family of students, teachers, parents, and staff. If you can, capture the memory of performances on video. With a video, even parents who couldn't make the actual performance can see their children shine. Video sales also help to raise some extra money for your school. At the O'Hearn, we always try to put the Talent Show (and all arts performances) on video. The arts teacher makes copies at the local public library and then offers them for sale to parents for $10. Typically, she will sell as many as 30 or 35 copies. Parents and students love having these as mementos of their shows.

Chapter 3

Parents Are Partners

In earlier chapters, we explored some of the ways we welcome and recruit parents, so that they are present and participating in a wide variety of events and activities at the O'Hearn School. Parents of our students often tell us how much they value the special, welcoming tone and feel of the O'Hearn—where they know that doors are open to them, that they will be respected, that their presence and contributions will be valued and appreciated. Yet above all of these aspects of parent involvement, above feeling welcomed, honored, and respected, the things parents value most are ways to support their children's academic development. In this chapter we explore four simple but powerful tools we have developed to help parents truly become partners in their children's education. These include:

I.   THE HOME READING PROGRAM
II. THE BOOK SWAP
III. THE AFTER-SCHOOL PROGRAM
IV. FAMILY MATH NIGHT

Partnering with Parents to Turn Reading Around

A home reading program gives parents a consistent, tangible tool to support their children's academic development.

In June of 1990, O'Hearn students' reading scores on the Metropolitan Achievement test placed them well below the national average, and near the bottom of the list of Boston's 78 elementary schools. Over ten years later, in 2002, O'Hearn students' scores on standardized tests placed them *first* among Boston's elementary schools. What accounted for this dramatic change? Clearly there are a variety of factors, but one that virtually all members of the O'Hearn community point to the school's home reading program.

In 1990, few O'Hearn students were doing significant reading at home. Now, close to 100% of students are either reading independently or being read to at least four nights every week! This is a direct result of the O'Hearn's home reading program, which has proved itself a powerful tool for boosting not only students' reading skills, but also their enthusiasm for reading. What's more, it has provided parents a tangible way to act as partners with teachers, and to support their children's learning.

The Home Reading Program

One way O'Hearn teachers have truly depended on parents as partners is the school's home reading program. This program also offers an opportunity for all families to be directly and consistently involved with supporting their child's learning. Regardless of their circumstances—despite physical, economic, or social barriers—virtually all parents truly want to be able to support their children's learning. A home reading program can be a wonderfully simple and powerful way for them to do just that. No doubt, reaching all parents is difficult, but our experience has shown that it is very much worthwhile. Here we highlight five key steps we followed in creating a successful home reading program at the O'Hearn:

The Steps

1. Create a home reading contract
2. Reach out to all parents
3. Support home reading from the classroom
4. Track data
5. Return to the hard-to-reach

1 Create a home reading contract

Students' low reading scores provide a clear indication that schools need to find ways to get students to spend more time reading. After trying a number of different strategies—reading contests, discount book sales, book giveaways—that did not yield significant gains, a team of teachers and parents at the O'Hearn developed a home reading contract. (*See Appendix, page 76.*) The team made sure that this contract had enough flexibility that *all* families could participate, whether they were working parents, parents of special-needs students, or parents for whom reading posed a significant challenge.

The simple contract established the school-wide expectation that students in kindergarten through second grade would read or be read to four nights a week for at least fifteen minutes, and students in grades three through five would do the same for at least twenty minutes. By allowing families to skip days, the home reading contract created flexibility for parents who have busy days or unexpected crises. The contract was also intentionally open-ended about who would do the reading. Students could read independently. A parent could read to them. And if a parent was unavailable or unable to read, a relative or friend could fill in. With these flexibilities built into the contract, the school-based management team was able to feel confident about expecting all parents to participate.

Each night, students record the title(s) of the book(s) and the number of minutes they read or are read to. Then their parents sign the contracts, to confirm that students have been doing this work.

2 Reach out to all parents

For a home reading program to be a real success, for it to have a real impact on achievement school-wide, aim for 100% participation. Don't just put a note in the school newsletter, suggesting parents participate. Don't just send letters home in students' backpacks. Don't just make an announcement to parents who show up at your fall open house. Don't just have teachers mention the program during parent teacher conferences. Do all of these and more!

Empower a team of parents to make home visits, where they can explain home reading to new parents, answer questions, and help come up with ideas for how even the busiest of families can participate. Equip this parent team with sample contracts and books they can give away. Equip them with books on tape for parents of students with special needs, and for parents who can't speak or read English very well.

At the O'Hearn, we identified a group of twelve parents to take responsibility for overseeing and supporting the home reading program. These

tips & ideas

Aim for 100%
Build in flexibility so 100% participation can be a realistic goal. At the O'Hearn, students can read or be read to. We also expect reading to occur four nights each week, not five.

Every Friday, kindergarten students choose new books for home reading.

tips & ideas

Empower parents to help other parents

Nothing overcomes barriers between schools and parents like other parents. Empower a team of parents as liaisons to oversee your home reading program and to provide encouragement to other families.

Stress teacher buy in

Add a home reading grade to report cards, and encourage teachers to ask follow-up questions about students' readings.

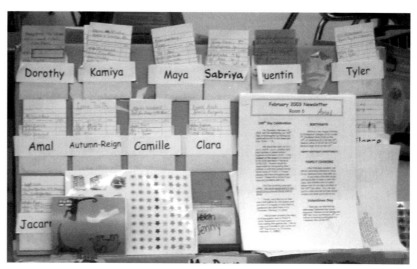

A simple bulletin board helps keep track of books students have read at home with their parents.

parents acted as liaisons between the school and the most "hard-to-reach" families. As our experience with home visits has shown us, nothing breaks down barriers between parents and schools quite as well as other parents.

3 Support home reading from the classroom

Another important feature of the home reading program at the O'Hearn is that all teachers support its implementation. Full participation isn't just mandated from the principal's office, all teachers expect it from all of their students. They collect and record students' reading contracts every week. They ask questions about books students are reading to check that they really are reading (and retaining what they read). All student report cards have a grade for home reading contracts. All of these pieces add up to reinforce for students that reading is important, and that teachers and parents are working together to help them get better at it.

4 Track data

Keep track of which students are turning in their home reading contracts, and how consistently they are turning them in. This data is important for many reasons. Over time, this data provides a clear picture of any positive impacts on students' reading skills (and scores). It helps you target those students and families who could use more support and encouragement. Over time, well kept data can also help you to pinpoint trends in which students are and are not participating—information that is useful for planning improvements to your program. At the O'Hearn, we also use data to help fuel the excitement about reading at our school. Parent liaisons create colorful posters for the "100% Club" and the "75-100%

Ms. Dawn helps a student pick her next home-reading book.

tips & ideas

Host special events for targeted families

Host special events for families of students who consistently do not participate in home reading. Let them vent frustrations and ask questions, then work together to come up with strategies.

Provide ongoing encouragement

Encourage parent liaisons to remain in contact with these families throughout the year for ongoing support.

Club," and they add the names of students who participate consistently in the home reading program. This way, even struggling readers can earn recognition and encouragement for their reading, which can motivate them to keep at it!

5 Return to the hard-to-reach

To meet, and to maintain your goal of 100% participation, do extra, ongoing outreach to parents and families that are persistently not participating. One fall at the O'Hearn, our parent liaisons hosted a pizza party just for the families of 35 children who were not participating in home reading. The parent liaisons extended personal invitations. They followed up with phone calls. They offered help with transportation. They emphasized that other children were welcome (so that child care would not be an issue or an excuse). Ultimately, 22 parents responded to this warm and persistent welcome. These parents were able to describe the challenges they were facing. Then the liaisons worked with them to come up with specific strategies. Some ideas that came out of this first discussion included: setting specific times and/or places for reading, restricting TV or video-game time, reading to several children at once, recruiting friends or relatives to help read, contacting teachers for appropriate reading materials, and calling each other for more ideas and help.

tips & ideas

Choose the right scale

Run a book swap at whatever scale(s) is right for your school. Start with teachers who are supportive and build each year.

Start a classroom book swap

A book swap can work at the classroom scale, the school-wide scale, or both at the same time. Classroom teachers can create a book swap of their own, with a collection of books just for kids in their room.

The Book Swap

A second key way that parents partner with the O'Hearn to support literacy is through a book swap. This simple practice serves two key purposes. It regularly gets books into students' hands and into their homes. It also provides a fundamental, recreational literacy activity for students. At the O'Hearn, the book swap is, quite simply, a whole bunch of books—by now about seven milk-crates' worth of books. These are kept on a rolling cart in a storage closet. Once every month, a parent takes this cart out, and creates a hallway display of books—organized by subject and by reading level. One classroom at a time, students visit the book swap, where they can leave a book and take a book (or two, or three, or more) for recreational reading. Six basic steps we followed to create a book swap are:

The Steps

1. Identify book swap coordinators
2. Start collecting books
3. Give books away
4. Develop a simple tracking system
5. Gradually build your collection
6. Acknowledge parent-leaders with stipends

1 Identify book swap coordinators

The first step in developing a book swap is to identify people who can share responsibility for it. At the O'Hearn, the book swap was initiated by the school's occupational therapists, in partnership with one parent, and a paraprofessional. Over time, one parent took primary responsibility for keeping the book swap going, and for recruiting new parent (and sometimes student) volunteers to help each month.

2 Start collecting books

Once you have identified book swap coordinators, start collecting books. Draw from as many different sources as you can think of. At the O'Hearn, the book swap book collection began with a request for book donations that appeared in the *O'Hearn Star*. The coordinators also distributed fliers, and made announcements at a variety of school events. The first batch of books was collected on a cart that began to make its rounds from classroom to classroom.

The book swap gets its first customers.

tips & ideas

Books set apart

Parents, be clear with your children about any books from your home collection that you don't want to have swapped. They just might disappear.

3 Give books away

Start your book swap with a book giveaway, so that all students can participate. Don't ever be stingy with books! At any day of the O'Hearn book swap, students who don't have a book can take one. If they bring one, they can take as many as they want.

4 Develop a simple tracking system

A book swap is not a library. Students don't have to fill out cards for every single book they take and read. Likewise, book swap coordinators don't need to keep track of exactly where every book goes. It is helpful, however, to develop a simple way to track how many books are being taken. This kind of information is very helpful when making the case for a book swap to possible funders. At the O'Hearn, the book swap coordinator keeps alphabetical lists of students in each class. When a student takes a book, she simply puts a check by their name, to keep a running tally of the number of books they take. This also allows the book swap coordinator to assess how well students are using this resource.

5 Gradually build your collection

Over time, the O'Hearn's collection of books has steadily grown. Using a small annual budget from a grant (about $500/year), the book swap coordinator builds the collection with monthly visits to Goodwill, where books sell for as little as fifty cents each. She also visits local libraries, which often have used book sales at the beginning of the year. Books left over from donations by programs like RIF (Reading is

tips & ideas

Don't swap at lunch

Lunchtime is too chaotic, with too much time, and too much else going on, making it easy for students to lose or misplace books. Set up in the hallway, where students can come in small groups from their classroom during a break time. They will spend as much time looking as you'll let them.

Fundamental) are incorporated into the book swap collection. As teachers clear books out of their classroom libraries, these can also be absorbed by the book swap.

6 Acknowledge parent leaders with a stipend

Wherever possible, acknowledge parent volunteers who make extraordinary contributions with a stipend. Verbal and written thank you's are important too. However, a stipend, even a small one, can demonstrate that you truly value a parent's time, their energies, and their talents. If your school is anything like the O'Hearn, your most devoted parents are often willing to dedicate long hours to the school, without expecting any payment in return. As the O'Hearn book swap has grown, it has become a more significant amount of work. Seeing firsthand the clear impact of the book swap on students' enthusiasm for reading (not to mention test scores), both teachers and parents wanted to recognize the hard work of the one parent leader who faithfully kept the book swap going. So, drawing on grants from the Annenburg Foundation, ReadBoston, and others, the O'Hearn offered an annual stipend to the book swap coordinator.

Swapping underway.

The After-School Program

tips & ideas

Every day, for two hours after school, four days a week, 160 days of the year, O'Hearn teachers and parents work side by side to run an after-school program. All parents with children in the program agree to volunteer at least once during the year—and many parents end up volunteering much more than that. The program is run by a parent and teacher co-director team, who, together with two lead teachers and four assistant teachers, are paid from a budget that is generated largely by parent-run fund-raisers. All of these features combine to make the O'Hearn after-school program a powerful tool for family involvement at the school. By working for the after-school program, either as volunteers, paid staff, or as an organizer of a fund raiser, parents become partners with the school, directly supporting students' social and academic development.

Start by assessing the need
Before you get down to the business of building an after-school program, administer a survey to parents to get a clear idea of the size and scope they are looking for.

The Steps

1. Administer a survey
2. Develop a plan
3. Develop a budget
4. Raise funds
5. Hire staff and recruit volunteers
6. Evaluate and improve

1 **Administer a survey**

As a first step, administer a survey of parents at your school to determine how many parents would want their children to participate and what they would like the program to look like. (*See Appendix, page 77.)* How many days a week should it meet? How long should it be? Should the focus be fun and socializing, academic enrichment and support, or some combination? Like many projects at the O'Hearn, the idea for an after-school program grew out of parent-to-parent conversations. Several parents of students with special needs were interested in creating an opportunity for their children to socialize with their peers and sharpen their academic skills beyond the regular school day. This small group of parents developed a simple survey to find out how many other parents would be interested, how many children might attend, how many days children would attend each week, how parents wanted the time to be

tips & ideas

Require parent participation

Help keep your adult-to-child ratio high by requiring parents of students in the after-school program to volunteer at least once each year. This provides extra "hands-on-deck," while helping parents appreciate all the work that goes into the program.

spent, and how much (if anything) parents felt they would be able or willing to pay for their children to participate.

As surveys came back from parents, it became clear that there was a wide interest in an after-school program. Originally conceived as an extension of the school day for special-needs children, the after-school program soon evolved into its current form, in which children who attend the school can participate.

2 Decide on logistics

After collecting and reviewing surveys, share your findings with the principal. Work together to decide on the logistics of your program. How many rooms will you need? How many rooms are available? What ratio of adults to children will you aim for? How many of these will be paid staff? How many will be volunteers? How late will the janitor(s) need to stay—and how much should the after-school program pay them for that extra time? Our principal recognizes that these kinds of ideas present opportunities to involve more parents as direct partners in educating their children. They are not excuses to create more responsibilities for an already hard-working staff.

3 Develop a budget

Once you have decided on the logistics of your after-school program—especially the number of paid staff you will hire and the length of your program—determine what your budget will be. In the 2002-03 school year, the O'Hearn after-school program ran for five days a week, two hours each day, for a total of 160 days. It was important to us that the after-school program operate on the same full-inclusion model as the rest of the school. This meant keeping the ratio of students to staff at six to one. In order to do this, we hired two "lead teachers" (who were paid $15/hour) and four "assistant teachers" (who were paid $11/hour). These six paid staff members were supported by a host of volunteers recruited from among school staff, parents, and the community.

4 Raise funds

With specific numbers in mind, work with your principal to estimate how much you will be able to bring in through enrollment fees, and how much you will need to raise through grants and other funding efforts. Don't worry about raising them all before getting started. At the O'Hearn, fundraising for the after-school program goes on all year. In some years, when fundraising has fallen short of our goals, we've just ended the after-school program earlier than the 160 days we aim for. In the 2002-03 school year, the O'Hearn after-school program operated with a budget of $23,680. Raising this much money was a challenge, but not an impossible one. About 25 percent came from fees (full-price for participation $30/week for each child, though we have a sliding pay-scale for lower-income families, so that all children can participate). Sixty percent came from a grant from the state Department of Mental Retardation. The remaining 15 percent came from parent-initiated fundraisers like the Talent Show, jazz night, bake sales, and yard sales—all of which double as opportunities to welcome, recruit, and partner with other parents and families. We will further discuss these kinds of parent-initiated projects in the final chapter of this book.

5 Hire staff and recruit volunteers

Once you've worked out all the details with your principal, once you've raised some funds, you're ready to hire staff and recruit volunteers. At the O'Hearn, the after-school staff consists of two co-directors (one parent and one teacher), two lead teachers, four assistant teachers, and as many volunteers as we can get—parents, paraprofessionals, and volunteers from the community. We also require that all parents of children in the program commit to volunteering at least one afternoon during the year—though most parents end up volunteering more than that. This is important for several reasons. It helps us keep the ratio of adults to children as high as possible. It gives parents a chance to see how much work goes in to running the after-school program. It also gives them valuable insights into how the program might be improved.

6 Evaluate and improve

As you run your after-school program, develop systems to evaluate and improve it year to year. Seek and welcome feedback and suggestions from parents, to assess your program's strengths and challenges, and to come up with strategies for making it better. Do this through ongoing, informal conversations, but also through more formal surveys, which your parents should complete at the end of each year. (*See Appendix, page 78.*) Drawing on suggestions from parents, the O'Hearn after-school program has continually grown and changed. It began as an idea for social enrichment for special needs students. Gradually, the program grew into a fully inclusive, social and academic opportunity for all students at the school. Our new goals for next year—adding a part-time nurse and a program developer/outreach coordinator—came directly from parent feedback.

tips & ideas

Seek, welcome, and respond to feedback

Seek, welcome, and respond to feedback from parents about how to improve your program so that it better meets students' needs. Do this informally, through ongoing conversations, and formally through follow-up surveys.

Go for it!

At the O'Hearn, when parents suggest a new idea or initiative to the principal, he hardly ever says, "no." More likely, they'll hear, "Sounds great. Go for it!" Notice, he doesn't say, "Great idea. I'll start working on it," or "I'll get my teachers working on it."

tips & ideas

Create many ways to be involved
Carve up responsibilities into many
bite-sized chunks, so that, no matter
how much time they have, parents
can take responsibility for something
manageable.

Family Math Night

Every March, O'Hearn students and their parents have the chance
to take part in Family Math Night. All of the classrooms are set
up with different math games. Volunteer parents and teachers
work alone or in teams to oversee the different games. The result is a fun,
social, educational event. Parents learn more about the math their kids
are doing in school, and also how to support them in their math work at
home. For a school without a lot of parent involvement, this kind of
event is another great launching pad, because it's so easy for parents to
get involved, either as a participant or as a volunteer.

The Steps

1. Recruit volunteers
2. Create math games
3. Involve everyone
4. Assemble take-home packet
5. Feed people
6. Have fun with math

1 Recruit volunteers

A Math Night offers a wide range of ways for families to be involved.
Use the school newsletter, notes in students backpacks, fliers posted
around the school, and word of mouth to recruit as many parent volunteers and participants as you can. Many parents will simply be present as
participants, playing math games with their children. Others may serve as
volunteers, taking on greater responsibility, possibly running or co-run-
ning (with a teacher or another parent) a math game in one of the classrooms. Whether parents are simply present and participating or taking
leadership roles, Math Night empowers them with specific knowledge
and skills they can use to support their children's work in math. At the
O'Hearn, Family Math Night is highly curriculum focused, so one or two
teachers typically take the lead in planning it. These teachers draw exten-
sively from a large pool of parent and teacher volunteers.

2 Create math games

Create a variety of math games students can play with their parents.
Speak with teachers to find out what skills they are working on with
their students. Work together to come up with ideas for relevant games

A map of the night's activities and data analysis in room 7.

tips & ideas

Let parents partner up
For some parents, involvement in a special event like Family Math Night will seem much less intimidating if they can work with a partner. Encourage parents to form teams with other parents or teachers.

that will help sharpen their skills. In one room, students might practice their measuring skills by jumping as far as they can, and using a ruler to see how far they went. In another, they practice estimation by guessing the number of marbles in a giant jar. In another, they do written calculations to decipher a cryptic message.

3 Assemble take-home packets

Equip parents with extra tools to support their child's math work even after Math Night is over. Assemble a packet of additional math games parents can play with their children once they go home. At the O'Hearn, parents who attend Family Math Night walk away with a large plastic bag of math-related goodies: a ruler, measuring tape, playing cards, stickers, a set of dice, and directions for a variety of math games they can play with their children. This packet also includes an excerpt from Megan Murray's *Schools and Families Creating a Math Partnership*, with ideas for parents such as, "Practice basic math facts," and, "Have high expectations and check on their progress often." One parent works with the school's lead math teacher to decide what should go into this packet. Then this parent recruits other parent-helpers to make copies and assemble them.

4 Involve everyone

Divide volunteer responsibilities into bite-sized chunks, so that parents won't feel intimidated about becoming involved. With a Family Math Night, parents can simply be present and participate, playing math games with their kids. They can bring food to help feed parents that didn't have

tips & ideas

Feed 'em!
If parents are already at school to pick up their child, don't make them go home and back again to fix dinner. Fix it for them.

Include special-needs students
Include a school store or a bake sale in Family Math Night, so that special-needs students can be part of the fun, interacting with parents and other students, and practicing simpler math skills, like counting money.

Art and math patterns in the cafeteria.

time to go home and cook before the event. Parents can be in charge of one of the math games, or they can help with setup or cleanup.

Make sure your Math Night also involves all students. Have different versions of games that are appropriate for students at different grade levels and abilities. At the O'Hearn, Family Math Night will also typically include a bake sale, the school store, or a smoothie-making, where special needs students—whose skills might not be advanced enough for games in the classrooms—can still participate and sharpen their mathematical skills.

5 Feed people
For an afternoon or evening event, be sure to make food available, especially for students who are already staying late for an after-school program. If parents are already planning to come to the school to pick up their child, don't make them go home and back again to fix dinner. Fix it for them, so you don't risk losing kids who are already at the school.

6 Have fun with math
Welcome parents as they arrive. Give them their math packet. Direct them to the food and to the various math games. At the O'Hearn, parents are greeted by parent volunteers, who set up a welcoming table right inside the front door. They receive their math packet and a map of the school that outlines what kinds of math games are happening in each room. After having some food in the cafeteria, parents and students set off to have fun with math.

Chapter 4

Parents Are Empowered

One of the most telling examples of parent involvement at the O'Hearn, is the large number of parents in leadership and decision-making roles at the school. In their landmark work, *Beyond the Bake Sale: An Educator's Guide to Working with Parents*, co-authors Anne Henderson, Carl Marburger, and Theadora Ooms assert that genuine, positive parent involvement almost always manifests itself in this way:

> *Any effective program to involve parents will probably lead to some parent involvement in decisions—about curricular emphasis, school programs, and discipline policy, perhaps even hiring and tenure. This is as it should be. Parents are not just extensions of their children; they are fully functioning adults who have important contributions to make. To attempt to confine their activities to bake sales and booster clubs is a tremendous waste of talent and energy—yours and theirs.*

In this next section we highlight two ways parents are given—and take on—leadership at the O'Hearn, one formal, and one informal. These include:

I. PARENTS ON THE SCHOOL-BASED MANAGEMENT TEAM
II. PARENT-INITIATED PROJECTS

tips & ideas

Invite multiple views

Don't let discussions be dominated by any outspoken teacher, principal, or parent, especially when discussing more contentious issues.

Don't dominate

As a principal, don't be overbearing. At the O'Hearn, after introducing the issues that need to be discussed and decided by the council, the principal leaves the room.

Parents on the School-Based Management Team

Many schools have some form of school-based management committee. At some schools, administrators or teachers hand-pick a few favorite parents—who may or may not be the best representative of other parents—to sit on these committees. At the O'Hearn, we open our school site committee to any parent who would like to be part of it, and we make a conscious effort to use this forum to truly empower parents, honor their insights, and harness their leadership skills. Following are five basic steps that help us do this:

The Steps

1. Welcome everyone
2. Accommodate all parents
3. Discuss and decide on a protocol
4. Set clear agendas
5. Facilitate, don't dictate

1 Welcome everyone

Schedule a first meeting and invite everyone—all parents, all teachers, and all school staff. Be clear that participation is voluntary and open to anyone who is interested. Make it clear that all parents and all teachers are welcome at all meetings, even if they are not voting members. Make a habit of distributing reminder notices and agendas at least one week ahead of time, so that anyone who is interested in the topics can arrange to attend.

2 Accommodate all parents

Make your school-based management meeting genuinely open to all parents by responding to the many different demands on parents' time and energies. Provide food and make child care available, so that working parents and parents with young children can attend. Otherwise, you may limit participation to parents from two-parent households who can afford babysitters. Vary the days and times of meetings. Hold some in the mornings, some in the afternoons, and some in the evenings, so that parents with different work schedules can attend.

Dr. Henderson welcomes parents at a parent meeting.

③ Discuss and decide on a protocol

Determine whether some parents and teachers will be voting members
all year, or whether different people will rotate in as voting members.
Develop a policy about voting—whose votes will count and with what
weight—that is aligned with your school's goals for parent involvement.
At the O'Hearn, each voting member has one vote, and a parents' vote
carries the same weight as the principal's vote, or a teacher's vote.

④ Set clear agendas

Set and stick to clear, concise agendas, so that you use parents' and teachers' time well. A school-based management meeting is not a forum for
wide-sweeping, philosophical discussions about education reform. Use
meetings to address specific, pressing issues, so that meetings can be productive, and participants can see concrete results.

⑤ Facilitate, don't dictate

Welcome multiple perspectives and viewpoints. Don't let a few outspoken
participants, even the principal, dominate discussion. Focus on facilitat-
ing an open conversation, where all participants can feel comfortable
expressing their honest opinions. At the O'Hearn, the principal presents
an overview of key issues but does not dictate discussion. In fact, after
introducing topics to be discussed, he often leaves the room, so as not to
dominate or exert undue influence on discussion. In this way, he also
demonstrates respect for those who might not otherwise share his views
on sensitive or contentious subjects.

tips & ideas

Give parents a voice and a vote
Demonstrate how much you value and
honor parents' input by making them
full voting members of school govern-
ing bodies.

Make it clear
Set very clear agendas and mail them
ahead of time. Advanced warning is
key. Make sure issues to be dealt with
are clear, so that meetings are productive and participants can see results.

tips & ideas

A Some schools rely too heavily on a few dedicated parents. At a school where parents are always welcome, veteran parent leaders can personally recruit and train new parents to fill their shoes well before they leave.

B Whether recruiting volunteers or new parent leaders, make time to talk about kids—they're the reason we're all here!

C When parents are empowered as part of school leadership teams, it increases the school's capacity to assess concerns and respond appropriately.

D By being willing to speak with parents on a walk-in basis, the principal makes it clear that families and their ideas are valued and respected.

Let Us Show You

PASSING THE BATON TO A NEW GENERATION OF PARENT LEADERS

It's a Wednesday afternoon in late September, the end of the school day at the Patrick O'Hearn. The hallways are teaming with activity. Ali Bledsoe, a veteran O'Hearn parent volunteer and leader, spots Danette Adams, a new parent whom she's been trying to recruit to help with the school's home reading program.

"Danette!" she calls, "How are you doing?"

"Hi, Ali. Great. It's good to see you. How are you doing?"

"Busy, busy, busy. You know me. I've been wanting to talk to you."

"Uh-oh."

"Don't be scared. I'd like you to think about taking some leadership of the home reading parent team next year. My son will be graduating from the fifth grade, so I will finally be moving on too." **A**

"Wow. I don't know."

"Don't give me an answer right now. Take your time. I'm going to talk to Kim Sprague, too. I really think the two of you would make a super team."

"Thanks, Ali. I'll definitely think about it."

"Great. Great. We'll talk. So, everything's OK? Your son is settling into first grade alright?" **B**

"Oh, he's fine," said Danette. "He just loves it here. Honestly, it's me having a harder time lately."

"How do you mean," asked Ali?

"Well…this new math he's bringing home. It's just so different from what I did in school. It's hard to know how to help him with his homework."

"I'm glad you mentioned that. I will definitely bring that up at the next school-based management meeting." **C**

"Great. Thanks, Ali!"

Before Ali left the school that afternoon, she stopped into Dr. Henderson's office.

"Dr. H. Hi. It's Ali."

"What's the word, Ali?" **D**

"The word is frustration, Dr. H."

"Frustration with what?"

"With this new math curriculum. Parents don't get it, and they don't know how to help their kids with it either."

"You have any suggestions?" asked Dr. Henderson.

"For starters, can we put it on the agenda for the next school-based

Patrick O'Hearn Elementary School
School Site Council Agenda for April 23rd, 2003

The next O'Hearn School Site Council Meeting will be held at the school on Wednesday, April 23rd, 2003, from 3:45-5:15 PM. All parents, teachers, and O'Hearn staff are welcome to attend. Please contact Ms. Scanlon in the front office by Tuesday, April 22nd, if you have any questions, and to let her know if child care is needed.

O'Hearn School Site Council
April 23rd, 2003, 3:45-5:00 PM Agenda

➤ Welcome

➤ Updates on:
    o Efforts to eliminate outdoor cigarette ads at nearby store
    o Arrangements with Mass. College of Art for participation in Peace Day Festival

➤ Scheduling of upcoming teacher / parent conferences

➤ Priorities for Whole School Improvement Plan

➤ School Uniforms

➤ Budget Reductions

➤ Elections of teacher and parent representatives for Personnel Sub-Committee

A sample agenda from a site council meeting.

tips & ideas

E By distributing agendas ahead of time, all families can know what issues will be discussed at school management meetings. This way, all interested families have an opportunity to participate.

F When principals facilitate, rather than dictate meetings, teachers and parents are empowered to take leadership on important projects.

management team meeting?"

"You've got it."

The following week, members of the school-based management meeting gathered for their monthly meeting. Several newer parents, including Danette, were there as well. They had seen that the math curriculum was on the agenda, and they wanted to add their voices to the discussion. **E**

Ali shared with the school-based management team the concern she'd heard from Danette and other parents.

Ms. McDowell, one of the teachers on the management team offered a suggestion.

"You know," she said, "this math is tricky. Teachers have been frustrated by it too. But we have also gotten a lot of training and coaching to help us figure it out. Would it be helpful to have a special math night just for parents? Teachers could do some sample problems with you, and give you some strategies. How does that sound?"

"Perfect," said Danette. "That's exactly the kind of thing I've been hoping for."

Hearing this, Dr. Henderson jumped in. "That sounds to me, Ms. McDowell, like you already have one eager parent volunteer. Am I right, Danette?" **F**

tips & ideas

G By including food and child care, many more parents may be able to attend school events.

H When getting the word out about school events, use as many forms of communication as you can, to reach—and include—as many parents as you can.

"Sure. OK. I don't know what I can do, but I can try."

"Wonderful," said Ms. McDowell. "You will be a great help to me."

"Anyone else like to pitch in?" asked Dr. Henderson.

Two more parents volunteered on the spot. Later, Ms. McDowell spoke to her teaching colleagues. Two of them agreed to help out, to stay late this one night for a special parent training. This planning team of teachers and parents met together one afternoon the following week to plan and divide up responsibilities. Danette offered to create a flier to send home in children's backpacks and to write an announcement for the *O'Hearn Star*. One parent offered to do child care, so that parents who couldn't arrange for babysitters could participate. The third parent offered to recruit a small team of parents to cook a pasta dinner, so that kids and their parents could eat before the math training. **G** The three teachers came up with ideas for sample math activities that would help parents understand the new curriculum and equip them with strategies for helping their children with math.

Three weeks later, after a note appeared in the *O'Hearn Star*, in students backpacks, and on the school calendar, over fifty parents came to the school for a special math night. **H** Many of them arrived still frustrated and confused by the new math curriculum. But they left empowered, equipped with specific tools and strategies to act as partners with teachers, able to help their children with their math.

Parents discuss plans for Math Night at a site council meeting.

Parent-Initiated Projects

In previous chapters, we have discussed a number of O'Hearn projects and events—the Talent Show, the after-school program, Math Night—that have been created and run by parents. In fact, we have only highlighted some of the most prominent examples. Parents do these kinds of things all the time at the O'Hearn, on many levels. At the O'Hearn, parents are not involved merely in projects and assignments teachers or administrators ask them to do. O'Hearn parents will recognize a need at the school and then take the initiative—administering surveys, forming committees, recruiting volunteers, assigning roles—to get things done. In the case of the Talent Show, parents recognized the need of a group of talented students who love to perform, matched with the almost unquenchable need of all parents to see their children be successful and their love of seeing their children onstage. Meeting this particular need led to a huge, school-wide event that now routinely sells out and raises hundreds of dollars for the after-school program. On a smaller scale, parents recognized a need for students to have more pleasure reading books, leading to a Book Swap. On a still smaller scale, parents recognized the need to give classrooms a new coat of paint, playgrounds some better landscaping, or teachers a special potluck lunch, to let them know how greatly they are appreciated.

This is the final section of this book, because we feel that parent-initiated projects are the fullest, most complete manifestation of family involvement. Parents have been welcomed, so that they are *present*. They have been recruited as *participants* at all kinds of school events. They have worked together with teachers and staff as *partners* in their children's education. They have been *empowered* as leaders within formal school structures like the school-based management meeting or the parent meeting. In a school where all of these things are happening, all the time, you create a fertile atmosphere for spontaneous eruptions of parent leadership.

What can schools do to empower parents as leaders, who will take this kind of initiative? This is a difficult question. In many ways, this is the kind of work that builds on itself—the more it happens, the more it happens. The more parents see other parents doing, the more new ideas they are likely to try themselves.

There may not be a precise set of steps teachers and administrators can take to compel parents to take more initiative. There are, however, a few

tips & ideas

Put money where your mouth is
Words of gratitude and appreciation are important, but for bigger, ongoing projects, offer stipends to parents, to recognize the value of their time. At the O'Hearn, parents often research and write grants to offer this support to volunteers.

tips & ideas

Keep them talking

Do whatever you can to keep parent-to-parent conversations going—provide phone and e-mail lists to all parents, publish a newsletter, create a family center, and host frequent special events to draw families together.

general principles we hold to, which yield a school-wide atmosphere where parent-initiated projects are possible—even likely. Here we highlight five of them:

The Steps

1. Empower parents from the principal's office
2. Refer to your parent-volunteer binder
3. Look for funding
4. Support ongoing communication
5. Accommodate all parents

1 Empower parents from the principal's office

Make your principal's office the launching pad for all kinds of parent-initiated ideas. Give parents the freedom to dream up, plan, and implement their own projects to support the school, specific teachers, and/or other parents. Encourage parents verbally. Be enthusiastic about new ideas, and follow through with logistical support. Make space available for parent meetings. If possible, help arrange for childcare and transportation, so that all parents can attend. Work with parents to develop budgets for their various projects, and brainstorm about possible sources of funding.

2 Refer to your parent-volunteer binder

The same survey you use at the beginning of the year to find ways for parents to support teacher-initiated projects can also provide a starting point for parents to initiate their own projects. Encourage parents to refer to the parent-volunteer binder to learn about other parents and the specific skills and interests they bring. Identify potential volunteers and speak with them directly about helping with your project.

3 Look for funding

For larger, more involved projects, look for funding, so that you can give stipends to parents who help out. Even if these are small, they are a clear demonstration of how much you value parents' time, skills, and contributions. The school budget might not have funding to spare, but work with your principal to come up with funding ideas, speak with teachers, and use your network of parents to explore possible grants from local community organizations, corporations, and foundations.

4 Support ongoing communication

The more parents are in communication with one another, the more creative and more empowered they can be to dream up, plan, and initiate their own projects. In the words of one O'Hearn parent:

> *Parent initiated projects can start in your kitchen, in the car, or on the phone. It's not just when you come in and have meetings. Any time parents get talking, they may realize, "Hey! We can do this! Let's have coffee and start hashing it out." And before you know it a project is underway.*

In addition to these informal, ongoing conversations, we encourage schools to consider communication tools and practices like those we use and have discussed in this book—such as a school newsletter and monthly calendar, so that all parents can be completely up-to-date on important events at the school; a parent-volunteer binder with information about parents skills, interests, and availabilities that is kept in the front office, so that all teachers and all parents can use this resource; school-based management meetings that are open to everyone; a family center, where parents can congregate, socialize, and dream up plans together; and a variety of events, traditions, and celebrations that bring parents to the school in great numbers, so that there are many opportunities for these conversations to happen. We are also developing a parent listserv, so that these conversations can continue via e-mail. As more and more of our families are connecting to the Internet, this is becoming a wonderful tool to help cultivate our families' connections with each other.

5 Accommodate all parents

When planning events, meetings, or any project where you'd like to involve parents, work to accommodate parents with a wide range of needs. Provide child care and food, and arrange carpools for parents and their children. This way, you welcome the participation of all parents—not just those from two-parent households, with their own car(s), or with money to spare for a babysitter. Even if e-mailed invitations, or notes put in students' backpacks lead to good turnouts at school events, aim for *great* turnouts by using every other form of communication you can think of—phone calls, posters, banners, letters, repeated reminders to students—to reach all parents.

tips & ideas

Provide carpools, child care, and food

Overcome three big barriers to participation by providing carpools, child care, and food. Not all parents have their own cars, a budget for child care, or the resources to attend an event and make dinner for their kids.

Appendix

WELCOME VISITORS!

After a brief introduction by the principal, you will have an opportunity to visit any of the classrooms listed on the other side of this form. These visits will be unescorted, we ask you to follow these guidelines.

DO:

Walk right into any classroom or instruction area that does not already have three visitors.

Go into the room along the side or back.

Observe what is happening in the room.

Talk with staff member only if approached by them.

Leave room when you want but spend no more than 20 minutes in one room unless otherwise arranged.

Leave messages or questions for staff in their mailboxes.

Ask principal any question you want.

DO NOT:

Go into any room that already has 3 other visitors.

Disrupt the students' learning.

Take pictures without prior permission.

Ask staff questions while they are engaged in teaching.

Thank you in advance

Parent Involvement Survey

There are many ways for parents to get involved at our school. We would like to get a sense of which projects you might like to participate in this year.

Following is a list of several projects parents have helped with in the past. Some of the roles parents played are noted in parentheses after each project.

Please review this short list, and place a check next to any project that is of interest to you—or any that you would simply like to learn more about. A teacher or parent leader will then contact you with more information. *Please note that you are only indicating your interest in learning more about these opportunities. You are not committing to be involved at this time.*

____ Family Center *(organize meetings, prepare food, welcome new families, invite speakers)*

____ School Newsletter *(collect articles, write articles, do format/layout, make & distribute copies)*

____ Bake Sales *(organize, bake goods, man table)*

____ Yard Sale *(donate sale items, price items, publicize event, man table)*

____ Home Reading Program *(introduce new families to program, support families struggling with system, administer awards program)*

____ Book Fair *(organize, publicize, man table)*

____ Talent Show *(recruit and organize talent, help with rehearsals, provide backstage help during production)*

____ Classroom Volunteer *(read, cook, photocopy, etc.)*

____ Plays/Musicals *(paint sets, sew costumes, help with rehearsals, provide backstage help during production)*

____ Other *(please describe)* _____

_____

Name _____

Child's Name _____   Room Number ____

Phone Number _____   Best time to reach you _____

A FLIER ANNOUNCING THE TALENT SHOW

FAMILY NIGHT DINNER / TALENT SHOW

Friday, May 2, 2003

Yes, its that time of year again. Auditions will be held on Monday, March 3 and Friday, March 7 from 3:30 to 4:30 pm. We are asking parents to encourage your children and children to encourage your parents to participate in this years show. Parents wishing to perform in the show do not have to come to the audition. They should contact Sharon Williams at ██████████

In past years, the shows have had a wide variety of performances: poetry reading, juggling, double dutch jumping, reading while standing on your head, gymnastics, singing, dancing, guitar, and piano playing. We have had mother and son, father and daughter, brother and sister, cousins, uncles, MBTA bus driver, school staff and spouses, and the principal perform.

This year's theme will be "Peace, Love & Happiness." We will be looking for musical performances that incorporate this them into their act.

While we encourage students to participate in the show, all students must be in good academic standing. Each student will need to have both his/her parents and teacher sign a permission form. Form must be returned by Friday, February 28, 2003.

The rehearsals for the show will be held every Monday and Friday starting March 10, 2003 from 3:30 to 4:30pm. Parents are responsible for making transportation arrangements for their children. All performers must be picked up by 4:40pm.

Tickets for the Show will be available in April. We encourage parents and friends to get their ticket as soon as possible. Seating will be limited. The price of the tickets for this event is $13.00 for adults and $8.00 for children.

All proceeds from this fund-raiser will go to the O'Hearn After-School Program to help sustain program affordability. The success of this event will depend largely on parents' cooperation in helping in any way possible. Parents interested in helping can contact Sharon Williams at 436-6439.

LOOK FOR MORE INFORMATION IN YOUR CHILD'S BOOK BAG.

Jazz Night

WE NEED YOUR SUPPORT!!

HELP SUPPORT THE PATRICK O HEARN FULL INCLUSION
AFTERSCHOOL PROGRAM BY ATTENDING OUR FAMOUS

JAZZ NIGHT!!!!

COME HEAR THE SOULFUL JAZZ SOUNDS OF THE
O HEARN COMMUNITY

Friday April 4th from 7pm to Midnight
at

Son's of Italy
120 Quarry St. Quincy Ma.

Great Food, Great Music, Great Company!!!

Ticket price:
1 @ 25$
2 @ 45$
4 or more 20$
(tickets may be purchased at the door for an additional 5$ per ticket)

Thank you!!   Hope to see you there!!!

THE O'HEARN HOME READING CONTRACT

HOME READING CONTRACT

Return By:

I, _____ will read or be read to for the time required by my grade level (15-20 minutes for K-Grade 2, or 20-30 minutes for Grades 3-5) For at least 4 days per week.

DAY 1:

Title of Book:_____

Minutes: ____

Parent Signature:_____

DAY 2:

Title of Book:_____

Minutes: ____

Parent Signature:_____

DAY 3:

Title of Book:_____

Minutes: ____

Parent Signature:_____

DAY 4:

Title of Book:_____

Minutes: ____

Parent Signature:_____

Patrick O'Hearn Elementary School

After School Program—*Interest Survey*

Several parents have recently expressed interest in creating an after-school program at the O'Hearn. This survey was designed to gather information about exactly what parents are looking for. Please take a few moments to complete it, to help the after-school program team build a program that reflects the priorities and needs of O'Hearn families.

For questions 1,2, and 3, please use the following scale:

5—Strongly Agree   **4**—Somewhat Agree   **3**—Unsure   **2**—Somewhat Disagree   **1**—Strongly disagree

1. I think the O'Hearn School should have an after-school program. *(circle one)*

   5   *4*   *3*   *2*   *1*

2. An after school program should focus on students' *social* development.

   5   *4*   *3*   *2*   *1*

3. An after school program should focus on students' *academic* development.

   5   *4*   *3*   *2*   *1*

4. If the school creates an after-school program, how many days/week would you like it to run?

5. If the school creates an after-school program, how many hours/day would you like it to run (i.e. what time should it finish)?

6. If the school creates an after-school program, how many of your children would you expect to enroll? Please also indicate the grade level of each child?

Name:_____   E-mail:_____

Phone:

The best way to reach me is*(check one)*: ☐ phone   ☐ e-mail   ☐ other:_____

Would you like to be part of the after-school program planning team? *(check one)*

☐ Yes! Please contact me with more information about how I can help.

☐ Maybe. Please contact me with more information.

☐ I don't think so.

Thank you!

Patrick O'Hearn Elementary School

After School Program—*Parent Survey*

This survey was designed to help assess how well the after school program is meeting the needs of our children and families. Please take a few moments to complete it, to help the parent/teacher after-school team to better serve you and your child.

For questions 1,2, and 3, please use the following scale:

5—Strongly Agree
4—Somewhat Agree
3—Neither agree nor disagree
2—Somewhat Disagree
1—Strongly disagree

1. Attending the after school program has helped my child improve socially. *(circle one)*

> *5   4   3   2   1*

2. Attending the after school program has helped my child improve academically.

> *5   4   3   2   1*

3. The after school program provided peer interactions in a supportive environment for my child?

> *5   4   3   2   1*

What changes would you like to see in the after school program next year, so that it better meets the needs of your child? Please give at least one specific example.

The Project for School Innovation

PSI is a grassroots network for public school educators to share their successes and drive school change. To strengthen and deepen this mission, PSI offers a range of services, including consulting, facilitation, public relations, and workshops and tools for educators to explore and implement effective practices.

Expanding the Use of Effective Practices

PSI explores the homegrown practices of successful public schools, helping them to find and share what works. PSI provides teachers and principals with action planning tools to replicate what they learn from their peers. By doing this, PSI brings effective practices to more children.

Promoting Teacher Quality and Leadership

PSI provides teachers with unique professional development and leadership opportunities. Through interactive, practice-based sessions, PSI helps teachers build key skills. By working with teachers to lead workshops and author publications, PSI increases teachers' confidence and commitment to the profession.

Cultivating a Culture of Innovation Among Educators

PSI brings educators from different schools together to engage in collaborative reflection and exchange. These activities build organizational learning, trust, and growth. Teachers are more receptive to new ideas when they come from their peers, and schools as a whole benefit from a culture of innovation.

I*ncluding Every Parent* is the eighth in a series of how-to guidebooks developed *By Teachers For Teachers* with support from the Project for School Innovation. Each guidebook in the *By Teachers For Teachers* series is based on the work of professional educators from successful public schools. (Given its subject matter, this book also drew from the expertise of a team of parents.) In a yearlong process facilitated and documented by PSI, these teachers identified, researched, and explored practices that make their school successful. To create this guidebook, the team generated step-by-step instructions other schools can follow to replicate each of these practices. Finally, they included dozens of tips and ideas, based on lessons they learned while implementing these practices at their school.

Customized Support

While each how-to guidebook serves as an excellent introduction to effective practices, additional customized training and technical assistance are available from the same teachers (and parents) who developed the book. To inquire about customized support, contact PSI by phone at 617-825-0703 or by email at psi@psinnovation.org.

Titles in the By Teachers For Teachers Series

1. *Measuring Success One Student at a Time: Tips and Ideas on Formative Assessment Practices*
Neighborhood House Charter School

2. *Including Every Child: Tips and Ideas on Effective Inclusion Practices*
Patrick O'Hearn Elementary School

3. *Create Your Own KidLab: Tips and Ideas to Make Science Engaging, Imaginative and Fun*
Neighborhood House Charter School

4. *Building Character: Tips and Ideas to Build School Climate that Fosters Student Achievement*
Academy of the Pacific Rim

5. *Skills for Success: Tips and Ideas to Turn Struggling Students into Confident Learners*
City on a Hill

6. *Reflective Learning: A Step-by-Step Guide to Fostering Critical Thinking in Young Students*
Cambridgeport Community School

7. *Calculated Success: A Step-by-Step Guide to Balanced Math Instruction that Works*
Roxbury Preparatory Charter School

8. *Including Every Parent: A Step-by-Step Guide to Engage and Empower Parents at Your School*
Patrick O'Hearn Elementary School

9. *No Longer At Risk: A Step by Step Guide for Helping At-Risk High School Students Succeed*
Lowell Middlesex Academy Charter School

10. *Learning After School: A Step-by-Step Guide to Providing an Academic Safety Net and Promoting Student Initiative*
South Boston Harbor Academy